My Life Struggles

ROBERT L. PATTERSON

My Life Struggles

This book is written to provide information and motivation to readers. Its purpose is not to render any type of psychological, legal, or professional advice of any kind. The content is the sole opinion and expression of the author, and not necessarily that of the publisher.

Copyright © 2024 by Robert L. Patterson.

All rights reserved. No part of this book may be reproduced, transmitted, or distributed in any form by any means, including, but not limited to, recording, photocopying, or taking screenshots of parts of the book, without prior written permission from the author or the publisher. Brief quotations for noncommercial purposes, such as book reviews, permitted by Fair Use of the U.S. Copyright Law, are allowed without written permissions, as long as such quotations do not cause damage to the book's commercial value. For permissions, write to the publisher, whose address is stated below.

Printed in the United States of America.

ISBN   978-1-64552-212-6   (Paperback)
ISBN   978-1-64552-211-9   (Digital)

Lettra Press books may be ordered through booksellers or by contacting:

Lettra Press LLC
30 N Gould St. Suite 4753
Sheridan, WY 82801
1 307-200-3414 | info@lettrapress.com
www.lettrapress.com

Table of Contents

My Life Struggles: As A Black Man Living In White America 1

My Life Struggles: In the Denominational Religions 6

My Struggles: As A Member Of The Church Of Christ 9

My Struggles: As A Gospel Preacher 12

Starting The Congregation In Colt, Arkansas 18

Placed Membership With The East Side Church Of Christ, In Little Rock, Arkansas 21

Returning To The Congregation In Colt 23

Resigned From The Congregation In Colt, Arkansas 28

Placed Membership With: The College Heights Church Of Christ In Pine Bluff, Arkansas 30

Established: The North Little Rock Church Of Christ 36

Merger Of The North Little Rock; And The Marion Street Church Of Christ 40

Purchased Our Own Church Building 42

My Struggles: With The Men Of C.A.L.M. 44

Robert L. Patterson

Minister For: The North Little Rock Church Of Christ; Located At 1708 Highway 161, North Little Rock, Arkansas

I Am Just A Nobody, Trying To Tell Everybody, About Somebody, Who Can Save Everybody. Appealing To The Lost Souls, To Come To Christ, Through Preaching The Gospel Of Christ Behind Pulpits, Teaching Personal In Home Bible Classes, And Through My Book, Title: Yoking Up To The Gospel Plow To Learn About Jesus Christ: And Through YouTube, And Prayerfully Through The Publication Of This Book Also.

I Am Truly Thankful To The God Of Heaven, For Those Of You Who Have Helped, And Are Helping Me To Share The Gospel Of Christ, To As Many People In The World As Possible Through The Your Prayers And Your Support.

PERSONAL

Father: The Late William Elbert Patterson
Mother: The Late Irene Patterson
There Were 18 Children Born Into This Union

Marital Status

Married to a beautiful wife Thelma A.
Patterson, and we have 4 lovely sons

Religious Works

I am a Gospel Preacher/Evangelist and Personal work developer. I am the author of a book titled, **Yoking Up To The Gospel Plow To Learn About Jesus Christ;** I also teach the gospel of Christ on **YouTube**, You can view us on YouTube, At The North Little Rock Church Of Christ, You can also view us on YouTube by Scanning Our QR Code On Your Cell Phone.

Inspiration

One day I was sitting in my office thinking about all of my familiar friends of whom I have known for years, who seem to have forgotten me, as well as some of my kinsfolk. As I continue sitting there, I thought about **Bro. Marshall Keeble,** And **Mr. Nelson Mandela** of how they must to have felt when they went through all those horrendous things during their life time, because of their own countrymen and other critics, At that moment I realized that I was going through some of the similar things that they went through. Thinking about those men gave me the encouragement to take a stand, and to speak out to the world concerning some of the most troublesome and embarrassing state of affairs that I have went through and are going through in my life.

Introduction

The object of this book is to share my life struggles with all Gospel Preachers, Bible class teachers, and to all people of the world.

My prayer to God is that the readers of this book will gain strength and spiritual understanding that all Christians are to strengthen and to help one another in the kingdom of God, which is the church of Christ.

The Bible said, "31 And the Lord said, Simon, Simon, behold, Satan hath desired to have you, that he may sift you as wheat: 32 But I have prayed for thee, that thy faith fail not: and when thou art converted, strengthen thy brethren" Luke 22:31-32.

Paul said, "16 For though I preach the gospel, I have nothing to glory of: for necessity is laid upon me; yea, woe is unto me, if I preach not the gospel" 1 Cor 9:16.

Acknowledgments

Acknowledgement is said to be a confession of appreciation and compliment.

Therefore, I want to confess my true appreciation to the God of heaven for giving me the knowledge to read and to understand Christ and the Apostles' doctrine, and for the ability to relate to his people through the means of writing.

I want to give thanks to My Lovely Wife, Thelma Patterson, for her wisdom and her knowledge, having her working with me has been very inspirational, she have inspired me greatly and has been a very good colleague. For her; I am most thankful.

I want to give a special appreciation to My Daddy, Elbert Patterson for his instructions, and My Mother, Irene Patterson for her encouraging words of wisdom, and to the both of them for loving and teaching me and the rest of my brothers and sisters not to let what other people say to or about us to cause us to deviate from doing the right things.

My deep gratitude and indebtedness is to you the readers of this book: I truly hope that it will inspire you in a Godly way; to use this book as a guide to teach believers in Christ how to grow spiritually, and how to teach nonbelievers to believe in God and in Jesus Christ, and his church.

My Life Struggles: As A Black Man Living In White America

My Life Struggles begin in White America on June 7, 1948 in Somerville, Alabama. That particular Monday afternoon, my Mother struggled giving birth to me her seventh child, she gave birth to me without the help from a midwife or any other medical assistant, after I was born I started breathing and struggling around on my own, my Mother wrapped me up and kept me warm until the midwife came and cut the umbilical cord, and cleaned the both of us up.

Mother was born during the time when young girls became women at a very young age. She was married at the age of 14 years old to my father who was 19 years old. Mother was a tall slim woman with beautiful dark skin, she was a very strong yet a gentle woman, and during her life time God blessed her to give birth to 18 children which included two sets of twins.

I can still remember seeing Mother when we was out in the fields picking cotton in the fall of the year, how that she would lay some of her children on her cotton sack and pull them alone as she picked cotton trying to help her husband to support their children.

Mother was a very wise woman who knew how to take care of her house, she could take a Rabbit, Raccoon, Squirrel, or an Opossum and cook it to perfection and make it taste like a gourmet meal of the day, from one of your finest restaurants.

Solomon said, "1 Every wise woman buildeth her house: but the foolish plucketh it down with her hands" Proverbs 14:1.

Mother was the (Tabitha) of the neighborhood and the surrounding area, she would visit the sick and aid them in whatever way she possibly could.

My daddy was a tall slim good-looking man, he was a mild-mannered man who stayed out of other people's business, and he taught us to always listen to our Mother's advice.

Daddy was multitalented, he did many different things that excited me when I was a child growing up, and to see him doing those things influenced me to follow his examples, which I have done all of my adult life. One thing that I really enjoyed seeing Daddy do was the way that he treated all of his children the same. Daddy was a positive role model for his family, and he showed no difference between any of us. Daddy trained us to the best with all of his ability, and for that I will forever be thankful.

Daddy was a happy-go-lucky type person with the personality of a Saint. He was well loved and respected among his peers. Daddy was a happy young man with a lot of beautiful children that made him look very strong.

Daddy was truly a provider for his family, I can remember seeing him come home after a long hard day at work, after eating supper he would get those old carbide lights out and clean them up and go night hunting that would last sometime until way over into the night, I've seem Daddy go tight line fishing to provide for his family, I've seen and helped Daddy bring home government commodities for his family and others.
Paul said, "8 But if any provide not for his own, and specially for those of his own house, he hath denied the faith, and is worse than an infidel" (1 Tim 5:8).

I have never heard Daddy murmuring and complaining about anything, no matter how bad the situations may seem to have been at work, or in the community, he always kept his cool that was one of the most impressive things about Daddy that have influenced me all of my life.

When I was about 14 years old Mother gave birth to her last children, which was a set of twins, a boy and a girl, not long after their birth the boy died, during that time I saw Daddy, my Strength, my Hero crying, because of the death of his child, at that particular time in my life, I came to realize that there are some things that people have to struggle through in their life in order for them to maintain their own strength and sensibility, and even though Daddy was not trying to teach me at that moment, yet I learned a valuable lesson, that has stayed with me all of my life, I learned that when life knock you down fall on your back, because if you can look up, you can get up.

As time passed on, Daddy allowed me to stop working on the sharecropper's farm, he allowed me to work at a Steele mill in West Memphis, Arkansas, which was only a few miles away from where we lived, not long after, I left Arkansas and went to Cleveland, Ohio and live with one of my older brothers and his wife for a short period of time.

I left Cleveland, Ohio and went to live with my oldest brother, another in Geneva, Arkansas, better known as College Station, which was right outside of Little Rock, Arkansas. I got a job at one of the lumber companies, and I work there for quite a while. Then my oldest brother and I went and worked together at a local construction company, now that was the bomb, we enjoyed working together going from town to town meeting different people, I really enjoyed my older brother, because when I was younger the people called me; little O'Neal, which was my brother's name.

Everything was going great, until one day I was working on my car at my brother's house, when two men came up and told me to get out from under the car, so I came out and asked them what was going on, one of them said to me, O'Neal; you better get out of town before somebody kill you, I told him that I was not O'Neal, he called me a liar, at that time the other man said that I was not O'Neal, those men told me that I better get out of College Station before somebody kill me thinking that I was my brother, shortly after that incident, O'Neal and I discussed the incident and he tried to assure me that everything was all right. Soon after, I moved from O'Neal's house into a boardinghouse in North Little Rock, Arkansas.

Soon after I started working at one of the steel mills in Little Rock, things went fairly well until one day one of the employees played a practical joke on me, and I tried to kill him on the job, the supervisor carried the two of us into the main office, and they began to question us on what happened in the plant, the other gentleman told his part of the incident, then after I explained my part of the incident, after a while they asked us both to leave the office for a few minutes, and then they call the both of us back in, and they said to me, Mr. Patterson, if I would apologize to the other employee then I could keep my job, I had never felt more humiliated in all of my life and at that moment, I told the manager to give me my check and my W-2 form, because I am sure that you all do not want me to come back to this plant ever again, and that is a promise, the manager then told the secretary to give me check, and my W-2 form. After leaving the plant I realized that I would have to struggle to maintain my livelihood, and my sanity trying to make a living in White America.

Shortly after that incident, I went to work at another tanking company in the Little Rock area, during this time I had moved from the boardinghouse in North Little Rock, to a nice duplex in the Little Rock area, my oldest sister was living with me at that time, and everything was going great, then one weekend a friend of our was in town visiting from Chicago Illinois, he had been to a party that lasted to long and he was too intoxicated to drive back to Chicago, so he ask me would I drive him back home, I said sure, I will drive you home.

After we got to Chicago, instead of me going right back to Little Rock, I decided to stay in Chicago for a while, my friend allowed me to live with him and his family, shortly after I went to work at a chemical company in West Chicago, again things was going good, I bought a car so that I could get around on my own. Soon after that I moved into my own apartment on the north side of Chicago on Francisco Street. I enrolled in a school of music to learn how to be a professional guitar player, guitar has always been my favorite musical instrument.

While living in Chicago I was initiated with a group of Masons, I truly enjoyed being a Mason, they gave us a book called look to the east, I was told to read and to learn it, every day for weeks I would read that manual, I would stand in front of a mirror practicing the hand signs, and the positioning of my feet, I studied those bylaws until I had them down pat, then they gave me a Masonic book that they call the Bible.

During that time I thought that I was on the right track religiously, I attended and participated in the regular Masonic meetings, I earned my degrees at the proper times, things was going good until I started questioning them concerning some discrepancies that I found in the Bible that they gave me: The problem that I had was that in the Masonic Lodge there is a seat that sit in the East of the lodge, and the man that set on it is called Worshiper Master, the members tried to explain to me that that was all right to do in their religion, I tried to explain to them what Christ said in the book of Matthew.

Christ said, "8 But be not ye called Rabbi: for one is your Master, even Christ; and all ye are brethren. 9 And call no man your father upon the earth: for one is your Father, which is in heaven. 10 Neither be ye called masters: for one is your Master, even Christ" Matt 23:8-10.

To my surprise, after I read these Scriptures to my Masonic brethren's, they still continued to hold on to their belief. After that I decided to leave the Masonic faith, and move back to Little Rock, Arkansas.

Of all the mistakes that Daddy and Mother may have made, and with all the faults that they may have had, Daddy and Mother; allowed me to teach them to become members of the church of Christ, and they did the best thing that any Father and Mother could do, they both died in the Lord: And I hope that their soul is resting in Abraham's bosom.

My Life Struggles:
In the Denominational Religions

After I move back to Little Rock, Arkansas, I joined a Missionary Baptist church, and shortly after I started working for one of the local railroad companies in North Little Rock, I was a member of the Baptist denomination for many years, and often times I would hear the Baptist preachers teach things that was contrary to the Scriptures, and sometimes they would teach that the members study the Bible for themselves.

So I read where the Bible said, "15 But sanctify the Lord God in your hearts: and be ready always to give an answer to every man that asked you a reason of the hope that is in you with meekness and fear" 1 Peter 3:15

The more that I searched the Scriptures for myself, the more inquisitive I became. I had grown to the point where I started asking preachers questioning concerning the Baptist religion, and about the things that were contrary to the doctrine of Christ, with the intent to get a Bible answer, but to the contrary.

I asked many Baptist preachers, why do Baptist preacher wear the title Reverend? When the Bible said, "Holy and Reverend is God's name.

The Bible said, "9 He sent redemption unto his people: he hath commanded his covenant for ever: **Holy** and **Reverend** is His Name" Psalm 111:9.

I also asked them about what Job said about giving flattering titles unto man.

Job said, "21 Let me not, I pray you, accept any man's person, neither let me give flattering titles unto man. 22 For I know not to give flattering titles; in so doing my maker would soon take me away" Job 32:21-22.

As time went by I had the privilege to meet with one of the Baptist preachers who taught in the school of preaching, in our conversation I asked him why is it that we play musical instruments in our worship to God, when God said to take it away from him.

The Bible said, "23 Take thou away from me the noise of thy songs; for I will not hear the melody of thy viols" Amos 5:23.

Paul said, "19 Speaking to yourselves in psalms and hymns and spiritual songs, singing and making melody in your heart to the Lord" Ephesians 5:19.

Doing that conversation I asked him, what are the Baptist preachers going to do about what Paul said to the Athens.

Paul said, "24 God that made the world and all things therein, seeing that he is Lord of heaven and earth, dwelleth not in temples made with hands; 25 Neither is worshipped with men's hands, as though he needed any thing, seeing he giveth to all life, and breath, and all things" Acts 17:24-25.

At that time the preacher stood up and said to me, Bro. Patterson, you are the boldest young man that I have ever met, and if you are not satisfied with the Baptist church, then I recommend that you go someplace else, he then said to me good bye. At that point I realized that I had found myself struggling in another religious dilemma.

I struggled for a long time in the religious denominational world, trying to find salvation for my soul. Then one day at work I met a young man name James, James had recently moved to Arkansas from Chicago, Illinois. Shortly after we became friends, he and his wife started going to church services with me at one of the local Baptist churches, they enjoyed the worship services that we had, after attending worship with me for a while, he said that he was thinking about joining the Baptist church where I attended, I hesitated for a moment, then I told him that I was going to be honest with them, and that I was not satisfied with the Baptist church, then I explained to him of the things that I had encountered with some of the Baptist preachers, I said to him that there have to be someone teaching the truth concerning the church where people can be saved. James continued his quest looking for a place for him and his wife to worship God, coincidentally one Sunday morning, James heard a man preaching on the radio telling people of the five things that people have to do in order to be saved.

That following Sunday James went to the church that he heard on the radio, and on that particular Sunday he was baptized into the church of Christ. The following day at work James was telling me of his experience of becoming a Christian at the McAlmont church of Christ in North Little Rock, Arkansas. As he talked more about the people at the congregation and how loving and pleasant they were, he told me that the preacher was teaching concerning the denominational churches of the world and the churches of Christ, it was so astounding and breathtaking just hearing him I was so amazed and overwhelmed by my emotions, and before I could realize that there could be some repercussion from the preacher at the Baptist Church where I attended, I asked him would those people from the church of Christ come to the Baptist church and teach us about the church of Christ. On 11-04-1974, a group from the McAlmont church of Christ came over to the Baptist church where I attended and taught us the gospel of Christ, the infallible truth concerning Jesus Christ and his Church. That same night, I and some others members of the Baptist church were baptized into the McAlmont church of Christ.

My Struggles: As A Member Of The Church Of Christ

Not long after I became a member of the church of Christ, I started working with the congregation doing personal work such as, door knocking, passing out flyers, and attending home bible classes in various homes, after doing that for a while, I realized that I wanted to be a personal worker, teaching, and bringing people to the church.

During that time, the McAlmont congregation had two 66 passengers school buses that was in need of repair, so I ask the preacher if I could repair those buses and use them in our personal work program, his reply was that the church could not afford to get them repaired, then and I asked him would it be all right if I repaired them at my own expenses, and he said yes.

So having the green light I went to work disassembling both of those engines and carry the parts to my shop where I cleaned and repaired the old parts, after the parts was cleaned and repaired I carry them back to the church building and installed the parts to both of those buses. After the buses were repaired, me and another brother in Christ named Ernest, went to the work driving those buses on a bus route that I had set up for the church, that bus driving program became a great success, we ran the buses to our yearly V.B.S (Vacation Bible School), gospel meetings, first Sunday's fellowship meetings, and on many other occasions, we were bringing in over 100 people on those two buses each Sunday for worship services. By the grace of God and with the help of all the members, the McAlmont congregation grew to the point of having two Sunday morning services.

After we got the bus ministry running and doing good, The preacher made me a Bible class teacher, and when I started teaching bible classes at the congregation, I was so excited that it felt like a light went off inside of me at that moment, because teaching was my childhood desire, and to be a teacher of the word of God was so exciting. I worked hard to learn the scriptures; I immediately read my bible three times from Genesis through Revelation. I made myself some pocket cards with scriptures on them so that I could read them while I was at work.

After being a Bible class teacher for a while, one of the deacons in the congregation met with me in his office, and he asked me did I know that the preacher and one of the elders had been listening outside of my classroom door for the past few weeks, I said no, I did not. A few Sundays later that particular elder came in and visited my Bible class for the next few weeks, then one Sunday he asked me did I want to be a preacher, I said, no sir; he said to me Bro. Patterson you are a very good Bible teacher, and you are sound in the doctrine, and I believe that you would make a very good gospel preacher.

A few weeks later the preacher asked me if I wanted to be a preacher, I said well I have not thought about it, he said you are a very good teacher, and I believe that you would make a good gospel preacher. Shortly after that conversation the preacher started a preacher's seminar where he taught me and a group of young men how to study the bible, and how to remember scriptures, and how to prepare sermons and the different type of sermons.

After completing the seminar, I started teaching home bible classes, God blessed me so wonderfully sometimes I would baptize from 5 to 6 people out of one class, and in one class I baptized a husband and his wife. One day at work my boss and I was riding in one of the company trucks, we was having a conversation about the church and being baptized into the one church, as I was teaching him he ask me could he be baptized today, I answer yes you can, he told me that he believed what I was teaching him and that he wanted to be baptized, I then turned the truck around and carried him to the McAlmont church of Christ and baptized him. The Lord continued blessing me over the next few years baptizing and bringing many people into the church through the power of God.

Truly I thought that everything was going great until one day, I went to serve the buses and one of them was missing, so I asked the preacher did he know what happen to one of the buses he said yes, he told me that they gave it to the Lewis Street congregation.

After that the preacher started saying in his sermons that some people can split the church, after hearing that for a few times, I asked one of the deacons of the congregation what does the preacher mean by splitting the church? he said to me, are you really that naive, I told him that in the Baptist church where I came from I never heard preachers talking about splitting the church, he then told me that the preacher was talking about me, so I asked him why would he say that about me?

The deacon said, you see Bro. Patterson, because you have baptized so many people here, that he believe if you decide to leave and start a congregation someplace else, those people that you have baptized will follow you, and that would cause a split in this congregation, I immediately told that deacon that I had no desire to become a preacher, nor do I have any desires of leaving the McAlmont congregation.

A few weeks later, one Sunday morning the preacher ask me to come into his office, and he told me about a congregation of the church of Christ in Forrest City, Arkansas, that needed a preacher, and he suggested that I should take that work, because he believe that I would do a good job down there with those people.

My Struggles:
As A Gospel Preacher

In 1983, the preacher of the McAlmont church of Christ, carried me to a church meeting that was held at the Scott Avenue church of Christ in Forrest City, Arkansas, where they were meeting to select a gospel preacher for that congregation, after the preachers and members finished discussing several things they hired me to be the preacher for that congregation, and after receiving the right hand of fellowship from the Ministers and the members of the Scott Avenue church of Christ there in Forrest City, I never saw the preacher from the McAlmont church of Christ, in Forrest City ever again, at that time I realized that my religious struggles as a gospel preacher had just begun in the church of Christ.

After I was carried to preach the gospel of Christ, at the Scott Avenue church of Christ, the preacher that carried me to that congregation never came back to that congregation as long as I preached there. At that point I thought about what Paul told Timothy.

Paul said, "16 At my first answer no man stood with me, but all men forsook me: I pray God that it may not be laid to their charge. 17 Notwithstanding the Lord stood with me, and strengthened me; that by me the preaching might be fully known, and that all the Gentiles might hear: and I was delivered out of the mouth of the lion. 18 And the Lord shall deliver me from every evil work, and will preserve me unto his heavenly kingdom: to whom be glory for ever and ever. Amen" 2 Tim 4:16-18.

A few weeks after I became the preacher for the Scott Avenue church of Christ, there was a meeting held with me and some Caucasian preachers and with what they call leading brethrens, the meeting was to discuss my salary, during that meeting I learned that the previous preachers for the Scott Avenue church of Christ was receiving monies from various congregations in the area, even as far away as Memphis, Tennessee, so they proceeded to tell me about the amount of money they will be paying me for preaching at that congregation, after hearing them and seeing what that recommendation was, I politely as possible said to those men that was in that meeting, brethrens I believe that I serve the same God that you serve, and I believe that the God that bless white people, will bless black people also, thank you for your generous offer, but until this congregation learn how to stand on its own feet, and learn to give and to support their preacher financially, we will have to do the best we can on our own little money, and on my railroad salary.

Paul said, "34 Yea, ye yourselves know, that these hands have ministered unto my necessities, and to them that were with me. 35 I have shewed you all things, how that so labouring ye ought to support the weak, and to remember the words of the Lord Jesus, how he said, It is more blessed to give than to receive" Acts 20:34-35.

Paul said, "10 Therefore I take pleasure in infirmities, in reproaches, in necessities, in persecutions, in distresses for Christ's sake: for when I am weak, then am I strong. 11 I am become a fool in glorying; ye have compelled me: for I ought to have been commended of you: for in nothing am I behind the very chiefest apostles, though I be nothing. 12 Truly the signs of an apostle were wrought among you in all patience, in signs, and wonders, and mighty deeds. 13 For what is it wherein ye were inferior to other churches, except it be that I myself was not burdensome to you? forgive me this wrong" 2 Cor 12:10-13.

I told the members of the Scott Avenue church of Christ, that I will work with my hands to help the congregation to grow to the point of being self-sufficient, I also told the congregation that we were not inferior to other churches, and that I would not be a burden to them, that is the stand that

I will take all of my life for the church, I told the congregation that we will work and wait until our changes come.

After I became the Minister for the Scott Avenue church of Christ, We hired a contractor to repair the front yard so that people could park their vehicles without getting stuck in the mud. We removed a small window air conditioner unit that was in the auditorium, and installed a central air conditioning unit for the entire building. We added a large kitchen and dining area and two Bible classrooms on to the back of the building. We also remodeled the auditorium, installed two new bathrooms at the front of the auditorium, and installed a new baptistery.

We bought a (56) passenger school bus for our personal work, I started a teacher's training class, I wrote Bible class books for new converts, I started a bible training class so that our teachers could learn how to teach the new converts, I started a Saturday night Bible study. We had different types of programs that our young people participated in. Over the next few years the congregation grew from 20 to 25 members to over 120 members, and we became the largest black congregation in the Delta area at that time.

The Scott Avenue congregation was doing good and growing very well, and during that time a gospel preacher from a congregation of the church of Christ the Marianna, Arkansas said, that I was drawing members from their congregation, which was not the case at all, their members would come and visit us at various times because at that time we were having Saturday night Bible classes, and members of other congregations would attend on those nights. Our Saturday night Bible class had grown in attendance to over 110 people. Unfortunately, the preachers in the surrounding areas were not satisfied with the progress that we was having at the Scott Avenue church of Christ.

To my honest unexpected surprise, the preachers in the Delta area, was informing the preachers in the Little Rock, and in North Little Rock, and in other areas of the progress that we were making at the Scott Avenue church.

One day I was contacted by the preacher of the McAlmont church in North Little Rock, we met in his office and we discussed the work that we were doing in the congregation at Scott Avenue, he informed me of the alleged problems that we were having, he also told me that because we had more members than the black congregation in Marianna have, that we had taking the prestige from them, I asked the preacher what do you mean taking prestige over another congregation, he told me that the largest congregation in an area have the precedence over the smaller congregation, I then said to him, this work is not about prestige, it is about saving souls, the thing that I thought that we all was working together in. In spite of that conversation, the congregation continued to grow.

After a few months had passed and the congregation was doing extremely well, we started talking about building another church building on Scott Avenue, after that rumored started going around the congregation saying I was trying to take the church from the family that owned the building, and some of the members started calling other preachers making false accusations against me, one preacher from the North Little Rock area churches of Christ, told them that the best way to get rid of a preacher was to get someone to accuse him of an immoral act. Soon after that, I was informed that some members of our congregation and members of other congregations was having private meeting in different members homes, discussing how to get me to leave the congregation.

On one particular Saturday evening a group of dissatisfied members called a meeting at the church building with many unfaithful members of the Scott Avenue congregation who had not been in worship in years, along with preachers and members from other congregations in the area, the preacher from the Akin Street church of Christ in Marianna, Arkansas, chaired the meeting, the preacher started by asking the congregations do anyone have anything against Bro. Patterson, there was a moment of silence and no one responded, then he asked again, at that time a women that was sitting with her husband stood up and came to the front, the preacher asked her have you ever had sex with Bro. Patterson, she said yes, and we both repented, she then return to her seat, the preacher then proceeded to tell the congregation, that even if Bro. Patterson repented, you have the right to not let him preach here.

I am absolutely sure that the gospel preacher from the Akin Street church of Christ in Marianna, and those other gospel preachers that were present in that meeting, knowingly and willingly disregarded the three step procedures that Christ taught the apostles concerning the withdrawing of fellowship from a member, therefore it appeared to me that those gospel preachers was not there to clear up the rumors, and to make the congregation better, but rather to make things worse, by totally disobeying the doctrine of Christ.

The Lord said, "15 Moreover if thy brother shall trespass against thee, go and tell him his fault between thee and him alone: if he shall hear thee, thou hast gained thy brother. 16 But if he will not hear thee, then take with thee one or two more, that in the mouth of two or three witnesses every word may be established. 17 And if he shall neglect to hear them, tell it unto the church: but if he neglect to hear the church, let him be unto thee as an heathen man and a publican" Matt 18:15-17.

All gospel preachers should know and teach that offences will come, and they should know that the Bible teach how to resolved those problems.

The Bible said, "1 Then said he unto the disciples, It is impossible but that offences will come: but woe unto him, through whom they come! 2 It were better for him that a millstone were hanged about his neck, and he cast into the sea, than that he should offend one of these little ones. 3 Take heed to yourselves: If thy brother trespass against thee, rebuke him; and if he repent, forgive him. 4 And if he trespass against thee seven times in a day, and seven times in a day turn again to thee, saying, I repent; thou shalt forgive him. 5 And the apostles said unto the Lord, Increase our faith" Luke 17:1-5.

The very next day which was Sunday morning, we started our service as usual, when suddenly there came a group of dissatisfied members into the church building interrupting the Sunday morning bible class, these men and women entered the church building like a group of vigilantes, one man had a long stick in his hand, one man had the print of a pistol in his pocket, this gang also was lead by the preacher from the Akin Street church of Christ in Marianna, Arkansas, they was telling me that we could not worship in this building, I tried to calm the situation down but it only got worse, it got to the point that the man that had the pistol in his pocket said to me, Bro. Patterson, if you preach here I will kill you myself. At that time one of the members asks me would I come and teach at their home in Colt, Arkansas, the Lord blessed me and some other members to leave the congregation that Sunday morning without anyone getting hurt.

Men and brethren, one of the most troubling things that I experience while I was preaching for the Scott Avenue church of Christ in Forrest City, Arkansas was the time when I received an invitation to come to preach on a Labor Day fellowship meeting that was to be held in Evanston Illinois, which is right outside of Chicago. When the preacher pick me up from the airport, he told me that he had received a phone call from the preacher of the McAlmont church of Christ, which told him not to let me preach in his pulpit. After the meeting was over in Evanston, an older gospel preacher that was at that meeting said to me, Bro. Patterson, I want you to tell the preacher of the McAlmont church of Christ that I said when he put you out; he put out a great gospel preacher. Shortly after I came back home from Illinois, I went to the preacher of the McAlmont church of Christ home and talked with him and his wife, and as I was telling the preacher what the preacher in Evanston told me to tell him, but I could not remember the man name, then the preacher of the McAlmont church of Christ wife said to me, that his name is Bro. Gant, she said that he called them and told them what he had said about you, and the preacher of the McAlmont church of Christ never made a comment to me concerning what Bro. Gant had said about me at all.

Starting The Congregation In Colt, Arkansas

After the outburst in the congregation at Scott Avenue, the Lord bless us to leave there without anyone getting hurt, we went to Colt that Sunday and worship in one of the members home, we worship there for a while waiting to see if the confusion was dying down at the Scott Avenue church of Christ, after seeing that there was no resolve, we had a meeting with the Christians that was worshiping at Colt, and we decided to start a work in Colt, Arkansas. After we established the congregation in Colt, Arkansas, it started growing rapidly; we were baptizing people from the community and the surrounding area. And because we did not have a baptistery at that time we were baptizing people at the area congregations. On two occasions, we went to the Scott Avenue congregation to use their baptistery to baptize some people, but the brethren refused to allow us to use their baptistery to baptize these lost souls.

Peter said, "47 Can any man forbid water, that these should not be baptized, which have received the Holy Ghost as well as we? 48 And he commanded them to be baptized in the name of the Lord. Then prayed they him to tarry certain days" Acts 10:47-48.

It is absolutely ludicrous for any Christian, or any person that profess that they believe in God to refuse a gospel preacher from using their facility to baptize a believer into the body of Christ, as those Christians did.

Soon after I met with the preacher of the Landau church of Christ in Forrest City, he and I knew one another very well, and when I explained to him of the situation that we encountered at the Scott Avenue congregation, he gave me a key to their church building with his permission to baptize whenever we needed to.

After worshiping in the church of Christ in Colt, the Lord opened the hearts of the owners of the home and they sold the property to the church. Immediately after we purchased the property we started remodeling the house turning it into a church building, we remodeled the front of the house to look like a church building, we converted the living room area into an auditorium, and we converted the bed rooms into class rooms. God kept his grace and mercy over us and within the next few years he allowed us to build a large auditorium, with a baptismal, and two additional class rooms, the work was a great success. We also were broadcasting on live radio on Sunday mornings.

Unfortunately disaster struck again, I was informed that some of the brothers from the Scott Avenue congregation were taking picture of the work that we were doing in Colt, and was sending them to some of the preachers in North Little Rock, and the Little Rock area. During that same time the Scott Avenue church of Christ sent out letters to many of the congregations in the surrounding areas saying that I was out of fellowship, for causing division at the Scott Avenue church of Christ. The scripture does teach that a congregation can take disciplinary actions against their members, however a congregation has no disciplinary control over a person that is not a member of their congregation, which at that time I was not a member of that congregation.

The Scott Avenue church of Christ had no scriptural authority to withdraw fellowship from me, and should not have sent out those dreadful, misleading, and heart breaking letters. There were many times when I would think about how I was being scandalized and criticized by my own preacher, and preachers who I believed were my friends, it became very burdensome to me during those times, yet I was able to remember what Paul said to Timothy.

Paul said, "10 We both work and suffer reproach, because we trust in the living God, who is the Redeemer of all men, particularly of those that believe" 1 Tim 4:10.

After the turmoil got so great in the Delta area I decided to contact the preacher of the McAlmont church of Christ, he schedule a meeting with me and the Elders of that congregation, during the meeting I ask the preacher why did you take me to Forrest City in the first place? I said, did you not know those people, the preacher said to me, I wanted to see how long would it take you to find them out, then one of the Elders said to me, Bro. Patterson why don't you leave that work in Colt and come back to this congregation, so that you will not be accuse of splitting the church.

Soon after the meeting at the McAlmont congregation, I called a meeting with the Colt congregation, and told them of the distress that I was in, and the more I look for answers or solutions, I keep coming up empty handed, so I told the congregation that I believe that the best thing for me to do was to stop preaching for awhile, and maybe this turmoil will pass over, we all agreed and prayed for the congregation in Colt, leaving Bro. James Bradley as the preacher.

Placed Membership With The East Side Church Of Christ, In Little Rock, Arkansas

After leaving the congregation in Colt, my wife and I placed our membership at the Eastside church of Christ on E. 15th St. in Little Rock, under the leadership of the local preacher. It was great and I really enjoyed myself, he allowed me to teach Sunday morning and Wednesday nights Bible classes, and occasionally he would allow me to preach to the congregation.

Things was going very well so I thought, until one Wednesday night the preacher made a statement to the congregation that Bro. Patterson class was larger than his class, then he kind of laugh it off. Shortly after that statement was made, talk started going around that I wanted to take over the congregation; that is something that I would never even think of doing, after that night we found out that it was a lots of thing going wrong in the leadership. One day we were having a meeting at the church building to deal with the brethren concerning those issues, and there was some new converts in the building with us.

So I ask the preacher was he going to let those new converts stay in the meeting, he said yes, I said to him that it was not good for them to be in this meeting, due to the nature of the business that was going to be discussed, the preacher replied, they are going to stay, I said to him, if they are staying then I will be outside, because I will have no part in hurting those new Christians minds. A few minutes after the meeting started one brother came out and ask me to come back inside, because they were auguring and taking loud, I told him that I cannot go back in there and get in that argument, because God is not the author of confusion, and neither am I, then I gathered my things and left the building.

Paul said, "33 For God is not the author of confusion, but of peace, as in all churches of the saints" 1 Cor 14:33.

Returning To The Congregation In Colt

During the time that I preached for the congregation of the church of Christ in Forrest City, I lived in Sherwood, Arkansas, and I would drive approximately 96 miles to Forrest City.

And During the time that I preached for the church of Christ in Colt, Arkansas, I would drive approximately 120 miles to Colt, Arkansas. And because of the distance I would worship on Wednesday nights at one of the local congregations in the Little Rock or surrounding area. Fortunately at that time I was worshiping on Wednesday nights, at the Dixie church of Christ in North Little Rock, under the leadership of a renowned gospel preacher.

During that same time, some of the members from the Scott Avenue church of Christ in Forrest City, contacted the preacher of the Dixie church of Christ, along with some other gospel preachers, the minister from the Dixie congregation set up a meeting with me, and we met in his office, and he proceeded telling me of the phone call that he had received from various people, concerning me being out of fellowship with the Scott Avenue church of Christ, during that time the preacher and I had several meetings concerning the nature of those allegations, the preacher from the Dixie church of Christ had his secretary to make transcripts of some of the tape recordings and phone conversations that he had received from various members, and from some of the gospel preachers.

During another meeting at the Dixie church of Christ, the preacher ask me if he would set up a meeting with some of the gospel preachers, and leaders of the church, would I be willing to go before them and present the things that I had on the written manuscript, I said yes, he then asked me did I want him to represent me at the meeting, or did I want to represent myself, my answer was thank you, but I want to represent myself.

I was so happy to get an opportunity to speak for myself before those renowned men's of God, whom I thought was expert in all customs and questions, and wanted them to know the truth, for I remembered what King Agrippa said to Paul, and what Paul said to King Agrippa.

The Bible said, "1 Then Agrippa said unto Paul, Thou art permitted to speak for thyself. Then Paul stretched forth the hand, and answered for himself: 2 I think myself happy, king Agrippa, because I shall answer for myself this day before thee touching all the things whereof I am accused of the Jews: 3 Especially because I *know* thee to be expert in all customs and questions which are among the Jews: wherefore I beseech thee to hear me patiently" Acts 26:1-3.

Not long after that meeting, the minister from the Dixie church of Christ, drafted a letter and sent it to several congregations of the churches of Christ, making them aware that there will be a meeting held at the Brown Street church of Christ in Lonoke, Arkansas on November 12, 1988.

On November 12, 1988, there was a meeting held at the Brown Street church of Christ in Lonoke, Arkansas, There was Approximately 70 Brethren's who met from various congregations of the churches of Christ to rectify and retract the rumors and the misunderstandings about the withdrawing of fellowship from me, for allegedly causing division at the Scott Avenue church of Christ, during that meeting the preacher from the church of Christ in Dixie made it absolutely clear that a congregation cannot withdraw fellowship from a person that is not a member of that particular congregation, according to what Christ taught in Matthews 18:15-17.

Christ said, "15 Moreover if thy brother shall trespass against thee, go and tell him his fault between thee and him alone: if he shall hear thee, thou hast gained thy brother. 16 But if he will not hear thee, then take with thee one or two more, that in the mouth of two or three witnesses every word may be established. 17 And if he shall neglect to hear them, tell it unto the church: but if he neglect to hear the church, let him be unto thee as an heathen man and a publican" Matt 18:15-17.

After all of the evidence was presented, during the meeting that was held at the Brown Street church of Christ in Lonoke, Arkansas, it was determined by those brethrens that I was in fellowship with the churches of Christ, it was also made clear that when I decided to return to the congregation in Colt, Arkansas, I was under the leadership of the Eastside church of Christ, and the preacher from the Eastside church of Christ confirmed that I was not out of fellowship with their congregation, at that time the preacher from the Dixie church of Christ requested that a letter be written concerning that meeting, and he ask that it would be read and/or the congregations be notified that I was in fellowship with the church.

The meeting ended with a prayer thanking God for men who were able to come together and discuss major problems such as this, and still be in fellowship with one another, immediately after the meeting ended, the preacher from the McAlmont church of Christ came up to me and said, Robert stay out of trouble; my reply to him was; yes preacher you also, and the preacher from the Eastside church of Christ came to me and apologized for the confusion that I was involved in with the Scott Avenue church of Christ; Unfortunately many years later I found out that that letter was never read in most of the congregations, therefore the members continued to act as if though I was out of fellowship with certain congregations.

A few weeks after the meeting that was held at the Brown Street church of Christ in Lonoke, Arkansas, I called the preacher of the Lewis Street church of Christ in Little Rock, Arkansas. I ask him if I could meet with him and talk about what was going on in the church, he told me to come on over, we meet and I proceeded telling him of the things that I was going through being withdrawn from, and having to leave the work in Colt, he ask me, saying Patterson; did you do those things that they have charge you with? I answer no, he said; if you have sinned repent and ask God to forgive you, but if you have not sinned, then you stand and do the work that God have given you to do, he said to me, doc you go back to Colt and build that congregation the best that you can, with the help of the people that God will give you, He said, Patterson, if I would leave a congregation every time someone lied on me, or cause me to suffer persecution, doc, I would have been gone from here, and you better believe me. He said to me, do you remember what Peter said in 1 Peter 5:10?

Peter said, "10 But the God of all grace, who hath called us unto his eternal glory by Christ Jesus, after that ye have suffered a while, make you perfect, stablish, strengthen, settle you" 1 Peter 5:10.

Bro. James also said Doc, don't forget what Paul told Timothy; in 2 Timothy 3:12.

Paul said, "12 Yea, and all that will live godly in Christ Jesus shall suffer persecution" 2 Timothy 3:12.

During that conversation Bro. James, the preacher of the Lewis Street church of Christ said to me, Bro. Patterson it is your time to suffer persecution for the cause of Christ. At that time I made up my mind to return to Colt, and to continue that work.

Soon after I left the Little Rock area and returned to the work in Colt, all of the members received me joyfully, and we work together in harmony for many years. Not long after I returned to Colt, I received an invitation from a congregation in West Memphis, Arkansas, inviting me to come and preach for their gospel meeting, but before the meeting took place, the brethren from the Scott Avenue congregation contacted the congregation in West Memphis, in an attempt to prevent me from preaching at their congregation.

During that time the preacher from the Southside church of Christ in Blytheville, Arkansas heard of what the brethren at the Scott Avenue was attempting to do against me, he set up a meeting with me and the brethren from the Scott Avenue church of Christ, during the meeting the minister explained to the brethren from Scott Avenue, concerning the things that they were saying about me; the preacher said to them these things that you all are saying about Bro. Patterson needs to be dropped, because you have no proof that those things are true, the brethren from the Scott Avenue church of Christ completely refused to listen to what that preacher had to say, so the preacher closed the meeting with a prayer.

Resigned From The Congregation In Colt, Arkansas

After working for the church in the Delta area for over 18 years, and seeing that the turmoil and hatred was sturdily increasing in many of the congregations that was in the Delta and other areas, I decided to resign from preaching the work, not realizing the repercussion that I would receive from God; I seem to had forgotten what God did to Jeremiah.

Jeremiah said, "9 Then I said, I will not make mention of him, nor speak any more in his name. But his word was in mine heart as a burning fire shut up in my bones, and I was weary with forbearing, and I could not stay. 10 For I heard the defaming of many, fear on every side. Report, say they, and we will report it. All my familiars watched for my halting, saying, Peradventure he will be enticed, and we shall prevail against him, and we shall take our revenge on him. 11 But the LORD is with me as a mighty terrible one: therefore my persecutors shall stumble, and they shall not prevail: they shall be greatly ashamed; for they shall not prosper: their everlasting confusion shall never be forgotten" Jer 20:9-11.

After leaving the congregation in Colt, I returned to the North Little Rock area and placed my membership with the 15th St. church of Christ in North Little Rock, under the leadership of the local preacher, I worship at that congregation for a great period of time, I became a Sunday morning and Wednesday night Bible class teacher, and occasionally the preacher would allow me to preach sermons from the pulpit, I started working with the personal work group, the elder of the congregation that was over the personal work group, he and I worked really good together as a team on that program, we started talking about ways of expanding the congregation and helping it to grow.

Soon after we started talking about buying a large bus so that we could bring in more people, not long after that the congregation bought a real nice bus so that we could go out and work the community and bring in young people and others to our worship services, shockingly to both of us before we used that bus for the first time, we were told to get rid of it, the elder got with the preacher I don't know what all transpired, but the elder return the bus back to the company that he bought it from.

After we got rid of the bus, the elder informed me that there was some discrepancy among some of the men of the congregation concerning the progress that we was engaged in, in the meantime the preacher had a meeting with me in his office about the situation that he was getting into, because of the work that we were doing, he said to me, I really appreciate what you are doing, but some of the brethren think that you are taking the congregation to fast, my reply to him was, how can you take the congregation to fast if God is in the plan? His answer was, yes, but I have to work with the brethren, I thanked him for his honesty and for allowing me the opportunity to work with him at their congregation, and I informed him that I would be moving my membership, because I was not there to cause any type of trouble at all, I ask him to pray for me and my wife, and we moved our membership from that congregation.

Placed Membership With: The College Heights Church Of Christ In Pine Bluff, Arkansas

After leaving the 15th St. church of Christ, in North Little Rock, my wife and I placed our membership at the College Heights church of Christ, in Pine Bluff, Arkansas, under the leadership of the local preacher, Pine Bluff is about 100 miles from Sherwood, the preacher and the members of the College Heights congregation received us with open arms and with warm open hearts.

After being at College Heights for two or three weeks, the preacher and I was talking one day and he told me that he had received a phone call from a preacher in the Little Rock area, asking him was he about to retire from preaching, and his answer was no, then he asked the preacher from Little Rock, what was he talking about, the preacher from Little Rock said, well I hear that Patterson is up there with you, also I heard that he was coming up there to take over that congregation, the preacher at College Heights told the preacher from Little Rock, that Bro. Patterson has not caused any trouble up here with me at all.

When we started worshiping at the College Heights congregation, I felt real comfortable and relieved from the stress of trying to get along with gospel preachers. Furthermore the preacher at the College Heights congregation had been a longtime friend of our family, the preacher and I had known each other, and each other families before either of us became gospel preachers, he and I had been longevity as friends.

The preacher took my wife and I through a Bible training class, after completing the class, he assigned us to teach Bible classes. Soon after I started teaching Sunday mornings and Wednesday night Bibles classes, we started having personal in home Bible studies, we started a personal work group, which consisted of door knocking and passing out flyers, inviting people to come to our worship services, also asking people if they would like to have a Bible study in the privacy of their own homes. We also help to revive the nursing homes visitations.

On Sundays after the morning worship service, after eating lunch, a group of members would get together and go to different nursing homes and sing to the people that lived in those homes, after singing there for a while, we received permission from the nursing homes to teach the gospel to those people, and doing so I became the teacher for the nursing home visitations.

During that time the preacher and his wife open their doors of hospitality to my wife and I, they gave us the privilege to live in their home on Sundays while we worship at their congregation, so that we would not have to make that long drive from Pine Bluff to Sherwood, my wife and I lived with the preacher and his wife for over three years, we had a hallelujah good time, it was like a kid running loose in Hershey's candy company, are it was like what David said.

David said, "1 Behold, how good and how pleasant it is for brethren to dwell together in unity" Psalm 133:1.

If you could imagine what it feels like to have people to laugh with in your face, and those same people criticizing and lie on you behind your back for a long period of time, and you finally find someone that had compassion on you, then maybe you can understand how I felt being in the presence of the preacher at the College Heights church of Christ.

David said, "2 It is like the precious ointment upon the head, that ran down upon the beard, even Aaron's beard: that went down to the skirts of his garments; 3 As the dew of Hermon, and as the dew that descended upon the mountains of Zion: for there the Lord commanded the blessing, even life for evermore" Psalm 133:2-3.

During one of our nursing home worship service after I had finished teaching my lesson, an old lady was there, she could not speak well, and she could not walk, she was crying and making loud noises as if though she was trying to say something, she had a son there, that was a member of the College Heights congregation, he tried to comfort her as much as he could, but the old lady continued crying and making loud noises.

So I asked her son could I talk with her, and he said yes. I kneeled down beside her and began to rub her hand, saying to her it's okay everything is going to be all right, that old lady calm down and started telling me the best that she could that she wanted to be baptized, then I ask her, do you believe what you have just heard, and the old lady said yes, then I asked her, do you believe that Jesus Christ is the son of God, and she said yes, then I asked her to say those words, the old lady said slowly, I believe that Jesus Christ is the son of God, then I told her, you must repent of your sins, and she said I repent of my sins, then I turned and asked those that was congregated at the nursing home, can anyone forbid water that this believer should not be baptized, there was a moment of silence because of tears of joy.

That same day we carried that old lady to the College Heights church of Christ building, where me and the old lady son, carried her up the steps and put her into the baptistery and I baptized her, the old lady son and I took her out of the baptistery, and some of the women took the old lady into the dressing room, and helped her to change her clothing, we all prayed giving God thanks for the new convert, and then we carried the old lady back to the nursing home, and the old lady son cried tears of joy, saying Bro. Patterson, I've been trying to get my mother saved for many years, he said Bro. Patterson, I truly thank you, and I said to him, let us give God the glory.

I have witnessed many things during baptisms, but I had never felt the power of the Holy Spirit like I did that day; the old lady son said that he had hoped for many years that there would be somebody to put his mother into the pool before it was too late, that baptism put me in mind of when John said in John 5:2-5, 7.

John said, "2 Now there is at Jerusalem by the sheep market a pool, which is called in the Hebrew tongue Bethesda, having five porches. 3 In these lay a great multitude of impotent folk, of blind, halt, withered, waiting for the moving of the water. 4 For an angel went down at a certain season into the pool, and troubled the water: whosoever then first after the troubling of the water stepped in was made whole of whatsoever disease he had. 5 And a certain man was there, which had an infirmity thirty and eight years. 7 The impotent man answered him, Sir, I have no man, when the water is troubled, to put me into the pool: but while I am coming, another steppeth down before me" John 5:2-5, 7.

Things was really going great at the College Heights congregation, Bible classes and worship services attendance was growing, we were baptizing people out of the home Bible classes, we encouraged many young and old people to come back to the congregation who has strayed away. My wife and I would drive from Sherwood to Pine Bluff, 3 to 4 times a week to teach in home Bible classes that were held in different member's homes.

During that time the rumor that I was out of fellowship with the church of Christ in Forrest City, had crept up in a meeting that was held by a group of Gospel preachers and other male members in the Central Arkansas area, the group was called C. A. L. M. Which stood for Central Arkansas Leadership Meeting? The preacher from the College Heights congregation asked me to start coming to those meetings with him, and perhaps those brethren will receive me into their fellowship. So I attended those meeting for a few months, and I found out that those men was meeting and discussing how to rule the congregations, and how they could get them to raise money for what they call a disaster relief fund, those men of C. A. L. M. was so devious that they agreed to go to the first Sunday Fellowship's, and raised money from the congregations that was represented, and that money could to be used to help other congregations that was in need.

I am absolutely persuaded according to the Scriptures that one congregation ought to help another congregation in times of need, my question to those men of C. A. L. M. was; was the money that Paul took to the church in Jerusalem was it for a disaster relief?

Paul said, "24 Whensoever I take my journey into Spain, I will come to you: for I trust to see you in my journey, and to be brought on my way thitherward by you, if first I be somewhat filled with your company. 25 But now I go unto Jerusalem to minister unto the saints. 26 For it hath pleased them of Macedonia and Achaia to make a certain contribution for the poor saints which are at Jerusalem. 27 It hath pleased them verily; and their debtors they are. For if the Gentiles have been made partakers of their spiritual things, their duty is also to minister unto them in carnal things" Romans 15:24-27.

During the time that we worship at the College Heights congregation, a sister at the College Heights congregation, started making accusations to the preacher that I was teaching false doctrine in the home Bible classes, after she would talk with him, he would ask me to come into his office, and he would tell me what that sister was saying, and he told me not to worry about it, he said you know how some people are. Then a few weeks later, the preacher asked me to come into his office again concerning some things that the same sister was saying about the home Bible classes, then I asked the preacher what was going wrong, because you are attending those classes as well as she is, the preacher told me not to pay that sister any attention, then I asked him, why don't you talk to that sister and tell her to leave this alone if you are telling me that everything is alright.

That behavior went on with that sister for about two or three more weeks, so I told my wife that if the preacher call me into his office again over something that that sister have said, then I was going to resign from working and worshiping at that congregation, because I did not want to be labeled as causing confusion at College Heights. Then it happened again, when the preacher asked me to come into his office concerning what the sister had said, I ask him could my wife come in with us, he said yes, after he talked a little while about what the sister said, I proceeded to tell him that I was resigning our services and that we would no longer be worshiping at their congregation, we prayed, shook hands and departed.

A few weeks later I called the preacher at the College Heights church of Christ in Pine Bluff, and schedule a meeting with him, my wife and I met with him at his home in Pine Bluff, I told him that I wanted to start a congregation of the church of Christ, in Sherwood, he gave us his blessings, and prayed for the congregation that we was going to set up, and gave us the right hand of fellowship, we departed his home and we remain being friends.

Established: The North Little Rock Church Of Christ

The congregation of the North Little Rock church of Christ started Saturday, May 5, 2003, in the home of Robert and Thelma Patterson, at 1704 East Palomino Drive Sherwood, Arkansas, with 4 members, Bro. Robert L. Patterson Preacher/Evangelist, my wife, Thelma A. Patterson my oldest sister, Hazel Montgomery and my youngest sister, Charlean Patterson. The Lord blessed us with 12 baptisms, and 11 people placed membership with us, total membership 27.

Soon after we started The North Little Rock congregation in Sherwood, Arkansas, there was a congregation of the church of Christ in the Rose City area in North Little Rock, that the white brethren was moving out of, and they wanted to turn the church building over to someone that was a preacher of the church of Christ.

After finding that out I contacted those brethren, because we were in need of a church building, those brethren allowed me to come over and preach to them for a few weeks they was impressed with me and the group of people that came and supported me during those weeks of service. Those men had a meeting with me and they agreed to let me have that church building, then one of the Elders said, before we close this deal with Bro. Patterson, let us ask the preacher of the McAlmont church of Christ one more time do he want this building, because we have over the years tried to give it to him but he refused, shortly after the brethren met with me again at the Rose City church building, they thanked me for working with them for the past few weeks, and they told me that the preacher of the McAlmont church of Christ decided to take the building, and they signed it over to him for one dollar.

I could not phantom in my mind why would the preacher of the McAlmont church of Christ except the building in Rose City at this time, after knowing that they had offered it to me, then I thought, okay Robert, this is the same man that took you to preach at a congregation in Forrest City, Arkansas and then told the people of the McAlmont congregation that you left there on your own, I said this is nothing more than another one of his false dishonest acts that he have done against me.

At this point I was in such disarray trying to find answers to why would a person treat another person like this when they confess to be Brothers in the faith, then I realized what John said in 3 John 9-11.

John said, "9 I wrote unto the church: but Diotrephes, who loveth to have the preeminence among them, receiveth us not. 10 Wherefore, if I come, I will remember his deeds which he doeth, prating against us with malicious words: and not content therewith, neither doth he himself receive the brethren, and forbiddeth them that would, and casteth them out of the church. 11 Beloved, follow not that which is evil, but that which is good. He that doeth good is of God: but he that doeth evil hath not seen God" 3 John 1:9-11.

At that time I came to realize that the preacher of the McAlmont congregation was acting like Diotrephes did in 3 John, he acted if though he had the supremacy over many of the black gospel preachers in and around the Little Rock area, and what he would tell them to do, many of them would honored it to the fullest, but to the contrary I was not moved nor threatened by his potential authoritative control, even though I had to struggle with the leaders of the McAlmont church of Christ and his followers, I continue doing what I had to do for the cause of Christ and his church.

On Sunday, May 18, 2003, there was a preacher's meeting held at the McAlmont church of Christ in North Little Rock, during that meeting the minister of the McAlmont congregation made a statement that some man had come into town and started a new work called The North Little Rock church of Christ, he further stated that if he asked any of you to speak or help within the work he could not give his blessing, because they would be marked or labeled, because of working with The North Little Rock congregation.

On May 21, 2003, two of the brethren from the McAlmont church of Christ met with the preacher of the McAlmont church of Christ, in regard of the meeting that was held on May 18, 2003, that meeting was to make sure if they could support the work at The North Little Rock church of Christ, and they asked him was that work scriptural, and is it okay to support and help out with that work? These men had their questions in a written form, the local preacher did not answer them verbally, nor did he sign the written form. On May 24, 2003 the same two brethren asked the local preacher why did he not signed the form that they ask him to sign, the preacher reply was, I am not the Pope. And those two brothers gave me a copy of that letter, and I have it on file.

On October 4, 2003, I was informed in the areas Preacher's Leadership Meeting known as C.A.L.M. that was held at the 15th St. church of Christ in North Little Rock, I was told by those preachers to write a letter regarding the new work called The North Little Rock church of Christ, and meet with the leadership of the 15th St. church of Christ concerning that new congregation.

On October 5, 2003, I met with the leadership of the 15th St. church of Christ, as I was instructed by the brethren and members of C.A.L.M. at approximately 6:45 PM. they expressed to me that they could not take the official position as to whether or not other congregations will fellowship the work that we had started, they said that issue must be reserved for the leadership of each congregation, in light of what the Scriptures teach, regarding local oversight, they said, if there be any additional concerns please see one of the leadership. And I have a copy of this letter on file.

In 2004 the Lord blessed us to move out of our home to a large warehouse on Pike avenue in the North Little Rock area, we remodeled that building making it look like a church auditorium, we had a large auditorium, we built several classrooms upstairs, and we built a day care for the children, the Lord also blessed us with 29 baptism, and 10 people placed membership with us, 8 people move their membership, total membership 58, and total baptisms year-to-date 41.The Lord continued blessing us even in my struggles with C.A.L.M.

Merger Of The North Little Rock; And The Marion Street Church Of Christ

On September 9, 2012, 11 men met at The North Little Rock Church of Christ to discussed the merger of the North Little Rock church of Christ with the Marion Street church of Christ in Jacksonville, Arkansas during that meeting Bro. Walker, the preacher of the Marion Street church of Christ agreed that I would be the local preacher of the Marion Street church of Christ, and he would be the administrator over the work. On September 23, 2012, The North Little Rock congregation started worshipping with the Marion Street church of Christ in Jacksonville, Arkansas.

After we move in with the Marion Street church of Christ, the preacher asked me to wait a few weeks before he announced to the congregation that I was the new preacher of the congregation, I agreed, and we started working together as a congregation, we started by taking out their old church pews and replaced them with our newer pews, we remodeled the auditorium, we added an additional bathroom, we remodeled the kitchen area, we installed a double side door for the main entrance, and we also landscaped the front yard of the church building so that people could enter through the main entrance.

A few months after worshiping at the Marion Street congregation, the members from The North Little Rock congregation started asking me, when was I going to start being the preacher of the Marion Street congregation, I told them that the preacher and I had been discussing that very thing, and he told me that it would not be much longer.

The preacher schedule a meeting with the two of us, we met in his office at the church building, and he started telling me of a scheduled that he had made up with the days that I would be preaching, then I ask him who helped him to make out that schedule? He said that he did it himself, I said to him, that is not the deal we made when we was discussing making the merger of the two congregations, then he proceeded telling me that it was going to take him a little time before he can tell the Marion Street congregation about the transition the men had previously agreed on. So we follow the procedure for quite a while swapping out preaching from one to the other, then we started losing members from the North Little Rock congregation because they were not satisfied with the agreement.

So I asked the preacher could we meet, and during that meeting I explained to him that when we met at the North Little Rock church of Christ, on Pike Avenue, we discuss the merger of the two congregations, you made it plain to me and those men that you were too busy to be a preacher and that you wanted me to be the preacher of the congregation, but now it seems as though you want to continue to preach, I said which is your prerogative, the meeting ended with no resolve.

A few months' later things was still being done the same way, so I talk with the preacher and explained to him that for the sake of both congregations I had decided to move my membership from the Marion Street church of Christ. The very next Sunday I was scheduled to preach, and I made it known to the congregation that I would no longer be worshiping at the Marion Street congregation, in my salutation I expressed to them my deepest love, and I thank them for the time that we worship together, and when I ended my sermon I beaded them farewell.

Purchased Our Own Church Building

After leaving the Marion Street church of Christ the following week, the Lord blessed us to rent a real nice ex-military warehouse on Municipal Drive in Jacksonville, Arkansas. We moved in right away and started having worship services at our new location, when I said that we moved into a new location, I didn't mean that we took the church furniture that we carried with us to the Marion Street congregation, because we did not, we had lots of church pews and church furniture stored in a storage building that we had rented before we moved to Marion Street.

The Lord continued blessing us over the next few years there on Municipal Drive in Jacksonville. Then one day beyond my wildest imagination I received a phone call from a young man that was visiting a congregation on Highway 161 in North Little Rock, Arkansas, he told me that the brethren had made an announcement that particular Sunday, that they had made up their minds to sell their church building, he asked me was I interested in buying that building, I said sure, then he gave me the phone number of one of the members that I could contact and find out more about what their plans.

So I called that person and they put me in contact with the two men that was in charge of that congregation, I spoke with them and they met with me at the church building a few days later, they asked me of my reason for wanting to buy the building, I said to worship and serve the Lord in, and they expressed their concerns to me and agreed to sell us the building, they quoted me the price and I accepted it.

To my joyful surprise, while we were working with the bank getting the loan papers together, and waiting for the loan to be approved, and to get the property appraised, those two brethren gave me the keys to the building and assured me that we can start worship in their right away, and they would not discontinue any of the utilities, even the alarm system, until we have closed the deal.

And thanks; be to the grace of God, in April 2017, we purchased the church building on Highway 161.

Peter said, "6 Humble yourselves therefore under the mighty hand of God, that he may exalt you in due time: 7 Casting all your care upon him; for he careth for you" 1 Peter 5:6-7.

My Struggles: With The Men Of C.A.L.M.

On September 8, 2013, during a first Sunday Fellowship meeting, a preacher from one of the congregations in the C.A.L.M. area read a letter telling the congregations that I had sin against them, and they are not to have any fellowship with him, all of this was done before any of those preachers came and talked to me.

On November 6, 2013, at a first Sunday Fellowship meeting held at the Purdon street church of Christ in England, Arkansas, a group of C.A.L.M. preachers and brethren assemble themselves together outside of the church building and they marched into the building demonstrating to the members that they were in unity with one another, during that meeting one of the preachers who was in charge of the treasurer said, that I made a statement in our newspaper that he was mismanaging the money that C.A.L.M. have raised during those First Sunday fellowship meetings, I never made that statement in the newspaper nor to anyone else.

In January 2015, some people ask me to come to Pine Bluff, Arkansas, and teach some in home bible classes, I accepted their invitation, then I called the Preacher of the church of Christ in Wabbaseka, Arkansas, and I told him that I was going to be teaching home bible classes in Pine Bluff area, and would he like to come and study with us, and help me to build up the congregations in that area, his reply was, that he did not want to get into that.

On January 31, 2015, we had our first in home Bible class, we had a very large turnout of people, and the Bible study went very well, when the class was over, a member of the College Heights church of Christ said, that he have something that he have wanted to tell me for years, he said to me before those people, that when their preacher was in his dying hours he called some of his brethren from his congregation together and told them that after he die, do not let Bro. Patterson be the preacher of the College Heights congregation, because if you do the other congregations will not fellowship with you.

It felt as though my heart fell to the floor from within me my fountain over flooded with tears. I felt humiliated, hurt, betrayed, and deceived, because in my heart I believed that I had found a very good friend who would stick close to me like a brother, and his passing was a great loss to me, after the man finished telling me of those things, he apologized to me and asked me to forgive him for not telling me sooner.

For over 6 years I had been telling people about this outstanding gospel preacher that I knew and had the pleasure of working with for over three years, only to find out that the friendship that I thought we had was only vanity and lies. After that conversation I could truly understand why neither preachers nor Christians knew that my honest intention was to work, teach and bringing people to the congregation where the preacher could preach the gospel to them, unfortunately that is not what they believed.

On Saturday evening, February 14, 2015, in Pine Bluff after the home bible class ended a brother from the College Heights congregation told me that during a business meeting that he had previously attended, he ask the brethren if the Saturday evenings classes that we were having become too large for the people homes, could we have the bible classes in the conference room at the church building, they answered positively no, they also stated that Bro. Patterson cannot teach in this building because he is not a member of this congregation.

One of the most astonishing things that happen at the College Heights congregation is that after the death of the local preacher, and after two other gospel preachers resigned from that congregation, two men of the congregation rose up and assumed the role of so-called leading brothers, those two men was self-appointed to be of the overseers of that congregation.

In 2015, a member from the Grand St church of Christ in Brinkley, Arkansas gave me a 19 page transcript of a telephone conversation between the gospel preacher of the church of Christ in Dixie, and several brothers from the Scott Avenue church of Christ; The chairperson of the telephone transcript told the preacher of the Dixie church of Christ, that the brethren from Scott Avenue were acting under the advice of the eldership, and the preacher of the McAlmont church of Christ, and the minister of the Eastside church of Christ, informed us to call a meeting with Bro. Patterson. These preachers gave the brothers at the Scott Avenue church of Christ in details of how to get rid of me from preaching at Colt, Arkansas.

On March 7, 2015, I attended a C.A.L.M. meeting held at the Airport church of Christ in Little Rock. During that meeting, I ask the chairperson would he give me a letter stating that I am in fellowship with the church, the chairperson stated that he would asked if a letter could be written to the fact that Bro. Robert L. Patterson is in fellowship with the church, he said that it was not protocol for C.A.L.M. to give him a letter and since none has been given in the past, there was no need to do so now, at that time, another brother stated that the use of letters in situation like these need to be watched very carefully, but Bro. Patterson and the North Little Rock church of Christ is in fellowship.

On April 11, 2015, I attended a C.A.L.M. meeting at the Airport church of Christ in Little Rock; I presented a written letter to the chairperson, asking him who was the president or head of C.A.L.M? I ask him was that meeting governed by a group of Gospel preachers and elders, I also ask him for a copy of their by-laws for my personal record. After the chairperson read the letter that I gave him, he answered saying, I am the chairperson, and C.A.L.M. does not have any by-laws, it is not a church function and it is not governed by the church.

How can it be that, that meeting was not governed by the church, when there was no one there but gospel preachers and brethren from various congregations of the churches of Christ?

During that particular meeting on April 11, 2015, a renowned gospel preacher made an announcement before the brethren, saying that he knew what the Bible teach about a brother who has a fault against another brother, but because we all are preachers, I am going to tell Bro. Patterson before you all that he is wrong and he should stop saying that I was stealing money from the church, after that meeting ended, I confronted that preacher, and I told him that I have always treated you right, and that I have always spoken highly of you, and that I have never once spoke down of you to anyone, I also told him to never again violate the scriptures, because we must always do what the word of God say, regardless of how we feel about it, after I reprimanded him; he repented, and asked me to forgive him, we prayed, shook hands, and departed.

Luke said, "3 Take heed to yourselves: If thy brother trespass against thee, rebuke him; and if he repent, forgive him. 4 And if he trespass against thee seven times in a day, and seven times in a day turn again to thee, saying, I repent; thou shalt forgive him" Luke 17:3-4.

C. A. L. M. is nothing more than a miss representation of the Central Arkansas Leadership Ministers, because there are many gospel preachers in the Central Arkansas area that are not even aware of the group who call themselves C.A.L.M. therefore C.A.L.M. is fraudulently representing some of the black gospel preachers in the Central Arkansas area.

Therefore I propose that all of the men who are affiliated with C.A.L.M. will renounce their involvement with that group of men, repent of their wrong doing, and make a verbal apology to all of the congregations that they are affiliated with in the C.A.L.M. area: Men of C.A.L.M. can't you see that there is enough confusion in the churches of Christ without the so-call-leaders of the church of Christ being involved in it? Men and Brethren let us never forget what Paul said to the church in Corinth, in 1 Corinthians 14:33.

Paul said, "33 For God is not the author of confusion, but of peace, as in all churches of the saints" 1 Corinthians 14:33.

Approximately 15 years after the meeting that was held in Lonoke, Arkansas, my wife and I went to one of the elder's home that was a member of the McAlmont congregation; I went there to ask him did they ever announce to the congregation that I was in fellowship with the church, and his answer was "I don't remember". During that meeting I could clearly understand why I have been treated as if though I have been out of fellowship all those years, it was simply because those so-called leaders of the McAlmont congregation announced that I was out of fellowship with the church, but they never announced that a meeting was held and those rumors and alleged charges against me had been cleared up, and that I was in fellowship with the church.

Men and Brethren: There are some Renegades gospel preachers who have deserted the gospel of Christ, and they refuse to accept the fact that on November 12, 1988, there was a meeting held at the Brown Street church of Christ in Lonoke, Arkansas, where there was approximately 70 Brethren's who met from various congregations of the churches of Christ, and they rectified and retracted the rumors and the misunderstandings about the withdrawing of fellowship from me, and at that meeting they made it clear that I was in fellowship with the church.

Now here we are; in September 2023, 35 years after the meeting that was held at the Brown Street church of Christ in Lonoke, Arkansas: men and brethren in September 2023, I had the privilege to talk with one of those Rebels a couple of times by phone, and he told me that if I would come to their C. A. L. M. meetings and get involved with their activities, and give a monthly two hundred dollar donation to their disaster relief fund, then they will fellowship with me: Now if I did that then I would become a Renegade Rebel the same as they are.

Table of Contents

The Great Fall Of The Devil: From Heaven 51

The Church Of Christ: Is The Kingdom Of God 57

The Church Of Christ: Is The Spiritual Place Of Defense 61

The Church Of Christ: Is Not A Denomination 65

Baptism: Makes People New 69

Bishops: Are Necessary In The Churches Of Christ In These Days 74

The Holy Ghost: Does Not Ordained Elders In The Churches Of Christ Since The Perfect Law Of Liberty Have Come 77

The Overseers Of The Churches Of Christ: In These Last Days 81

Modern-Day Women: Must Be Governed By The Written Word Of God 85

The Truth: Concerning Widows And Widows Indeed In the Churches Of Christ 91

The Truth: Concerning Funerals 95

The Truth: About Holidays 98

The Truth: About Christmas 100

The Truth: About Christmas Trees 104

You Can Shake It And You Can Make It 106

God Does Not Speak Verbally: To Men In These Last Days 110

What You Are Seeking: Is Seeking You 114

Children Of God: Live Your Dream 118

Stray Gospel Preachers 121

Gospel Preachers: Who Have Retired, Or Is Intending To Retire...... 124

Some Things That Satan: Has Sifted Out Of The People Of God.... 128

Black People History: In White America... 132

Walk Out On Faith 137

Black Christians Leaving: The Black Congregations Of The Churches Of Christ 141

Aliens: In A Strange Land 145

Learn Better: Do Better 149

If You Could Hear Of Christ Again... 154

Three Degree's Of The Devil 158

Brothers And Sisters 162

The Black Hebrew Israelites 166

Some Things That Christians Should Take Back From: The Devil.... 171

Illegal Use Of Alcohol And Drugs 176

God's Instructions: For The Forgiveness Of Sin 180

The Devil Wants To Deceive The Entire World To Believe, That The Great Commission That Christ Gave To His Twelve Disciples Was Given To All Gospel Preachers Who Live In All Of The Continents Of The World; And That Is Absolutely A False Deception. 185

Prayer Of Thanks... 187

The Great Fall Of The Devil: From Heaven

Before Satan great fall from Heaven, he had the privilege to go out and to come into heaven at his own will.

In Isaiah, you can read where he was questioning Satan concerning his great fall from heaven, Isaiah also referred to him as being called the son of the morning, signifying that he was something great in heaven.

Isaiah said, "12 How art thou fallen from heaven, O Lucifer, son of the morning! how art thou cut down to the ground, which didst weaken the nations! 13 For thou hast said in thine heart, I will ascend into heaven, I will exalt my throne above the stars of God: I will sit also upon the mount of the congregation, in the sides of the north: 14 I will ascend above the heights of the clouds; I will be like the most High. 15 Yet thou shalt be brought down to hell, to the sides of the pit" Isaiah 14:12-15.

After Satan and his angels was thrown out of heaven, they were so angry with God until one of his angels with his tail pulled down the third part of the stars out of heaven trying to get revenge against God.

John said, "3 And there appeared another wonder in heaven; and behold a great red dragon, having seven heads and ten horns, and seven crowns upon his heads. 4 And his tail drew the third part of the stars of heaven, and did cast them to the earth: and the dragon stood before the woman which was ready to be delivered, for to devour her child as soon as it was born" Rev 12:3-4.

Before Satan and his angels was thrown out of heaven, the scriptures prove that he had schemed up some devilish plans to prevent salvation from coming unto mankind, and to prevent the church of Christ from being established or built in the earth.

John said, "10 And I heard a loud voice saying in heaven, Now is come salvation, and strength, and the kingdom of our God, and the power of his Christ: for the accuser of our brethren is cast down, which accused them before our God day and night. 11 And they overcame him by the blood of the Lamb and by the word of their testimony; and they loved not their lives unto the death. 12 Therefore rejoice ye heavens, and ye that dwell in them. Woe to the inhibiters of the earth and of the sea! for the devil is come down unto you, having great wrath, because he knowing that he hath but a short time" Rev 12:10-12.

Satan and his angels are trying to recruit as many human beings they can, planning to make an attack and fight against the God of heaven in the last days.

John said, "13 And I saw three unclean spirits like frogs come out of the mouth of the dragon, and out of the mouth of the beast, and out of the mouth of the false prophet. 14 For they are the spirits of devils, working miracles, which go forth unto the kings of the earth and of the whole world, to gather them to the battle of that great day of God Almighty. 15 Behold, I come as a thief. Blessed is he that watcheth, and keepeth his garments, lest he walk naked, and they see his shame. 16 And he gathered them together into a place called in the Hebrew tongue Armageddon" Rev 16:13-16.

God, knowing that Satan and his angels was planning to use mankind to fight against him, so then God in his unforeseen wisdom made his earthly soldiers; a five pieces spiritual armor for them to wear, and a spiritual sword for them to use to fight against Satan and his angels.

Paul said, "13 Wherefore take unto you the whole armour of God, that ye may be able to withstand in the evil day, and having done all, to stand. 14 Stand therefore, having your loins girt about with truth, and having on the breastplate of righteousness; 15 And your feet shod with the preparation of the gospel of peace; 16 Above all, taking the shield of faith, wherewith ye shall be able to quench all the fiery darts of the wicked. 17 And take the helmet of salvation, and the sword of the Spirit, which is the word of God" Eph 6:13-17.

Paul said, "1 Thou therefore, my son, be strong in the grace that is in Christ Jesus. 2 And the things that thou hast heard of me among many witnesses, the same commit thou to faithful men, who shall be able to teach others also. 3 Thou therefore endure hardness, as a good soldier of Jesus Christ. 4 No man that warreth entangleth himself with the affairs of this life; that he may please him who hath chosen him to be a soldier" 2 Tim 2:1-4.

Christian's soldiers must use their inner ability to overpower Satan and his angels, they must use the strategy that they have learn from the word of God so that they can defend the doctrine of Christ and themselves so that they will win against the tactics of Satan, and they must never give up on fighting the spiritual warfare; making sure that Christians will have an entrance into the everlasting kingdom of Jesus Christ.

Peter said, "10 Wherefore the rather, brethren, give diligence to make your calling and election sure: for if ye do these things, ye shall never fall: 11 For so an entrance shall be ministered unto you abundantly into the everlasting kingdom of our Lord and Saviour Jesus Christ. 12 Wherefore I will not be negligent to put you always in remembrance of these things, though ye know them, and be established in the present truth" 2 Peter 1:10-12.

All Christian's should realize that the power of the Spirit of God that is in us is greater than the power of Satan.

John said, "4 Ye are of God, little children, and have overcome them: because greater is he that is in you, than he that is in the world. 5 They are of the world: therefore speak they of the world, and the world heareth them. 6 We are of God: he that knoweth God heareth us; he that is not of God heareth not us. Hereby know we the spirit of truth, and the spirit of error" 1 John 4:4-6.

All Christian's should follow the example of Michael the Archangel when he was competing with the devil concerning the body of Moses and never discuss anything with the devil unless it is to say get behind me Satan, or say devil, the Lord rebuke you.

Jude said, "9 Yet Michael the archangel, when contending with the devil he disputed about the body of Moses, durst not bring against him a railing accusation, but said, The Lord rebuke thee" Jude 1:9.

James said, "7 Submit yourselves therefore to God. Resist the devil, and he will flee from you. 8 Draw nigh to God, and he will draw nigh to you. Cleanse your hands, ye sinners; and purify your hearts, ye double minded" James 4:7-8.

God showed John what was going to happen in the end of the world.

John said, "17 And I saw an angel standing in the sun; and he cried with a loud voice, saying to all the fowls that fly in the midst of heaven, Come and gather yourselves together unto the supper of the great God; 18 That ye may eat the flesh of kings, and the flesh of captains, and the flesh of mighty men, and the flesh of horses, and of them that sit on them, and the flesh of all men, both free and bond, both small and great. 19 And I saw the beast, and the kings of the earth, and their armies, gathered together to make war against him that sat on the horse, and against his army. 20 And the beast was taken, and with him the false prophet that wrought miracles before him, with which he deceived them that had received the mark of the beast, and them that worshipped his image. These both were cast alive into a lake of fire burning with brimstone. 21 And the remnant were slain with the sword of him that sat upon the horse, which sword proceeded out of his mouth: and all the fowls were filled with their flesh" Rev 19:17-21.

The angel assured John that the Devil, and his angels, and his false prophets, nor any of his lying false gospel preachers cannot enter into the new Jerusalem by no means whatsoever; furthermore the angel assured

John that only those who names are written in the Lamb's book of life shall enter into the new Jerusalem.

John said, "10 And the devil that deceived them was cast into the lake of fire and brimstone, where the beast and the false prophet are, and shall be tormented day and night for ever and ever. 11 And I saw a great white throne, and him that sat on it, from whose face the earth and the heaven fled away; and there was found no place for them. 12 And I saw the dead, small and great, stand before God; and the books were opened: and another book was opened, which is the book of life: and the dead were judged out of those things which were written in the books, according to their works. 13 And the sea gave up the dead which were in it; and death and hell delivered up the dead which were in them: and they were judged every man according to their works. 14 And death and hell were cast into the lake of fire. This is the second death. 15 And whosoever was not found written in the book of life was cast into the lake of fire" Rev 20:10-15.

That old serpent call the Devil know for sure that he cannot go back to heaven on any terms whatsoever, therefore his anger is so great against God that he is trying with all of his power to prevent as many human beings as he possibly can from going to heaven, therefore he is constantly using a direct attack against God, but God summons an angel and sent him unto John assuring him and all that believe in him according to the doctrine of Christ, that everything was going to be all right in the last day, he showed him the church, the Lamb's wife, he showed him the New Jerusalem, he also showed him the 12 gates that was heavily guarded by 12 angels each.

John said, "9 And there came unto me one of the seven angels which had the seven vials full of the seven last plagues, and talked with me, saying, Come hither, I will shew thee the bride, the Lamb's wife. 10 And he carried me away in the spirit to a great and high mountain, and shewed me that great city, the holy Jerusalem, descending out of heaven from God, 11 Having the glory of God: and her light was like unto a stone most precious, even like a jasper stone, clear as crystal; 12 And had a wall great and high, and had twelve gates, and at the gates twelve angels, and names written thereon, which are the names of the twelve tribes of the children of Israel:

13 On the east three gates; on the north three gates; on the south three gates; and on the west three gates" Rev 21:9-13.

The Church Of Christ: Is The Kingdom Of God

The Spiritual Kingdom Of God: Is A Territorial Unit Ruled By God.

Daniel said, "44 And in the days of these kings shall the God of heaven set up a kingdom, which shall never be destroyed: and the kingdom shall not be left to other people, but it shall break in pieces and consume all these kingdoms, and it shall stand for ever" Dan 2:44.

The Devil: Tried with all his power to prevent Christ from being born, but with no avail.

John said, "1 And there appeared a great wonder in heaven; a woman clothed with the sun, and the moon under her feet, and upon her head a crown of twelve stars: 2 And she being with child cried, travailing in birth, and pained to be delivered. 3 And there appeared another wonder in heaven; and behold a great red dragon, having seven heads and ten horns, and seven crowns upon his heads. 4 And his tail drew the third part of the stars of heaven, and did cast them to the earth: and the dragon stood before the woman which was ready to be delivered, for to devour her child as soon as it was born" Rev 12:1-4.

The Devil: Tried to kill Christ when he was an infant, but with no success.

Matthew said, "12 And being warned of God in a dream that they should not return to Herod, they departed into their own country another way.

16 Then Herod, when he saw that he was mocked of the wise men, was exceeding wroth, and sent forth, and slew all the children that were in Bethlehem, and in all the coasts thereof, from two years old and under, according to the time which he had diligently enquired of the wise men. 17 Then was fulfilled that which was spoken by Jeremy the prophet, saying, 18 In Rama was there a voice heard, lamentation, and weeping, and great mourning, Rachel weeping for her children, and would not be comforted, because they are not" Matt 2:12, 16-18.

Before the church of Christ or the kingdom of God had been established, the devil tried with all his power to prevent Christ from building his church or his kingdom.

The Bible said, "1 The word that Isaiah the son of Amoz saw concerning Judah and Jerusalem. 2 And it shall come to pass in the last days, that the mountain of the LORD'S house shall be established in the top of the mountains, and shall be exalted above the hills; and all nations shall flow unto it. 3 And many people shall go and say, Come ye, and let us go up to the mountain of the LORD, to the house of the God of Jacob; and he will teach us of his ways, and we will walk in his paths: for out of Zion shall go forth the law, and the word of the LORD from Jerusalem" Isaiah 2:1-3.

Paul assured the Christians in the church of Christ at Colossae that the Devil could not prevent the kingdom of God, which is the church of Christ from being built or established in the world, so that all human beings will have the right to be a member of it.

Paul said, "12 Giving thanks unto the Father, which hath made us meet to be partakers of the inheritance of the saints in light: 13 Who hath delivered us from the power of darkness, and hath translated us into the kingdom of his dear Son: 14 In whom we have redemption through his blood, even the forgiveness of sins" Col 1:12-14.

The Bible said, "8 But unto the Son he saith, Thy throne, O God, is for ever and ever: a sceptre of righteousness is the sceptre of thy kingdom. 9 Thou hast loved righteousness, and hated iniquity; therefore God, even thy God, hath anointed thee with the oil of gladness above thy fellows" Hebrew 1:8-9.

Nebuchadnezzar said: The kingdom of God is an everlasting kingdom.

Nebuchadnezzar said, "1 Nebuchadnezzar the king, unto all people, nations, and languages, that dwell in all the earth; Peace be multiplied unto you. 2 I thought it good to shew the signs and wonders that the high God hath wrought toward me. 3 How great are his signs! and how mighty are his wonders! his kingdom is an everlasting kingdom, and his dominion is from generation to generation" Dan 4:1-3.

God said: That his Kingdom and His Word Cannot Be Shaken.

The Bible said, "24 And to Jesus the mediator of the new covenant, and to the blood of sprinkling, that speaketh better things than that of Abel. 25 See that ye refuse not him that speaketh. For if they escaped not who refused him that spake on earth, much more shall not we escape, if we turn away from him that speaketh from heaven: 26 Whose voice then shook the earth: but now he hath promised, saying, Yet once more I shake not the earth only, but also heaven. 27 And this word, Yet once more, signifieth the removing of those things that are shaken, as of things that are made, that those things which cannot be shaken may remain. 28 Wherefore we receiving a kingdom which cannot be moved, let us have grace, whereby we may serve God acceptably with reverence and godly fear: 29 For our God is a consuming fire" Heb 12:24-29.

All Christians: Should give thanks to God, for allowing us to be members of the kingdom of his dear son, Jesus Christ.

Paul said, "12 Giving thanks unto the Father, which hath made us meet to be partakers of the inheritance of the saints in light: 13 Who hath delivered us from the power of darkness, and hath translated us into the kingdom of his dear Son: 14 In whom we have redemption through his blood, even the forgiveness of sins: 15 Who is the image of the invisible God, the firstborn of every creature" Col 1:12-15.

All Faithful Christians: Should rejoice, knowing that when Christ deliver up the kingdom to God, we will go to heaven with him.

Paul said, "24 Then cometh the end, when he shall have delivered up the kingdom to God, even the Father; when he shall have put down all rule and all authority and power"1 Cor 15:24.

The Church Of Christ: Is The Spiritual Place Of Defense

Defense: Is the method or the act of defending or protecting against attack, danger, or injury.

America has a civil defense warning system that is sounded once a day to inform the people of a potential attack; so that if there was an actual attack the people will know where to go and what to do for defense.

According to the Bible: The House Of God Is A Place Of Defense; And The Bible, The Written Word Of God Give The Entire World Warning Against The Attack Of The Devil!

Jesus used chickens to demonstrate to his disciples: The real meaning of the Place of Defense.

The Bible said, "37 O Jerusalem, Jerusalem, thou that Killest The Prophets, and stonest them which are sent unto thee, how often Would I Have Gathered Thy Children Together, even as A Hen Gathereth Her Chickens Under Her Wings, and ye would not! 38 Behold, your house is left unto you desolate. 39 For I say unto you, Ye shall not see me henceforth, till ye shall say, Blessed Is He That Cometh In The Name Of The Lord" Matt 23:37-39.

David prayed to God: Asking him to be his Strong Rock, for a House of Defense.

David said, "1 in thee, O lord, Do I Put My Trust; let me Never Be Ashamed: deliver me in thy righteousness. 2 bow down thine ear to me; Deliver Me Speedily: be thou My Strong Rock, for An House Of Defence To Save Me. 3 For Thou Art My Rock And My Fortress; therefore For Thy Name's Sake Lead Me, and Guide Me. 4 Pull Me Out Of The Net That They Have Laid Privily For Me: for Thou Art My Strength" Psalms 31:1-4.

David said, "7 How Excellent Is Thy Lovingkindness, O God! therefore The Children Of Men Put Their Trust Under The Shadow Of Thy Wings. 8 They shall be Abundantly Satisfied With The Fatness Of Thy House; and Thou Shalt Make Them Drink Of The River Of Thy Pleasures. 9 For With Thee Is The Fountain Of Life: in Thy Light Shall We See Light. 10 O Continue Thy Lovingkindness Unto Them That Know Thee; and Thy Righteousness To The Upright In Heart" Psalms 36:7-10.

Jude pleaded with the gospel preachers: To see the importance of defending the Place of Defense.

The Bible said, "1 Jude, the servant of Jesus Christ, and brother of James, to them that are sanctified by God the Father, and preserved in Jesus Christ, and called: 2 Mercy unto you, and peace, and love, be multiplied. 3 Beloved, when I gave all diligence to write unto you of the common salvation, it was needful for me to write unto you, and exhort you that ye should earnestly contend for the faith which was once delivered unto the saints. 4 For there are certain men crept in unawares, who were before of old ordained to this condemnation, ungodly men, turning the grace of our God into lasciviousness, and denying the only Lord God, and our Lord Jesus Christ. 5 I will therefore put you in remembrance, though ye once knew this, how that the Lord, having saved the people out of the land of Egypt, afterward destroyed them that believed not" Jude 1:1-5.

Paul warned the brethren in Philippi: That there are some gospel preachers who are not defending the Place of Defense.

Paul said, "15 Some indeed preach Christ even of envy and strife; and some also of good will: 16 The one preach Christ of contention, not sincerely, supposing to add affliction to my bonds: 17 But the other of love, knowing that I am set for the defence of the gospel. 18 What then? notwithstanding, every way, whether in pretence, or in truth, Christ is preached; and I therein do rejoice, yea, and will rejoice" Phil 1:15-18.

Paul said, "19 For I know that this shall turn to my salvation through your prayer, and the supply of the Spirit of Jesus Christ, 20 According to my earnest expectation and my hope, that in nothing I shall be ashamed, but that with all boldness, as always, so now also Christ shall be magnified in my body, whether it be by life, or by death. 21 For to me to live is Christ, and to die is gain" Phil 1:19-21.

God made it known to the world: That the Place of Defense will never be destroyed.

The Bible said, "44 And in the days of these kings shall the God of heaven set up a kingdom, which shall never be destroyed: and the kingdom shall not be left to other people, but it shall break in pieces and consume all these kingdoms, and it shall stand for ever" Dan 2:44.

Jesus made it absolutely clear: The Devil in hell cannot stop him from building a Place of Defense for the people of God.

Jesus said, "18 And I say also unto thee, That thou art Peter, and upon this rock I will build my church; and the gates of hell shall not prevail against it" Matt 16:18.

Paul told the brethren in Ephesus: To prepare themselves with the whole armor of God, so that they can defend the Place of Defense.

Paul said, "11 Put on the whole armour of God, that ye may be able to stand against the wiles of the devil. 12 For we wrestle not against flesh and blood, but against principalities, against powers, against the rulers of the darkness of this world, against spiritual wickedness in high places. 13 Wherefore take unto you the whole armour of God, that ye may be able to withstand in the evil day, and having done all, to stand. 14 Stand therefore, having your loins girt about with truth, and having on the breastplate of righteousness; 15 And your feet shod with the preparation of the gospel of peace; 16 Above all, taking the shield of faith, wherewith ye shall be able to quench all the fiery darts of the wicked. 17 And take the helmet of salvation, and the sword of the Spirit, which is the word of God" Eph 6:11-17.

The Church Of Christ: Is Not A Denomination

Spiritual Divisions: Is The Act Or Process Of Dividing or The State Of Having Been Divided.

Paul Taught The Church Of Christ In Corinth That They Must Not Get Involve With Spiritual Divisions; Paul Knew That Spiritual Division Will Cause Denominationalism Among The People Of God.

Paul said, "10 Now I beseech you, brethren, by the name of our Lord Jesus Christ, that ye all speak the same thing, and that there be no divisions among you; but that ye be perfectly joined together in the same mind and in the same judgment. 11 For it hath been declared unto me of you, my brethren, by them which are of the house of Chloe, that there are contentions among you. 12 Now this I say, that every one of you saith, I am of Paul; and I of Apollos; and I of Cephas; and I of Christ. 13 Is Christ divided? was Paul crucified for you? or were ye baptized in the name of Paul? 14 I thank God that I baptized none of you, but Crispus and Gaius; 15 Lest any should say that I had baptized in mine own name. 16 And I baptized also the household of Stephanas: besides, I know not whether I baptized any other" 1 Cor 1:10-16.

Paul explained to the brethren in Corinth: That he had to speak to them on a child level, because they were still Carnal.

Paul said, "1 And I, brethren, could not speak unto you as unto spiritual, but as unto carnal, even as unto babes in Christ. 2 I have fed you with milk, and not with meat: for hitherto ye were not able to bear it, neither yet now are ye able. 3 For ye are yet carnal: for whereas there is among you envying, and strife, and divisions, are ye not carnal, and walk as men" 1 Cor 3:1-3.

Paul explained to the brethren in Corinth: That they must avoid being called by the names of men, because that is what caused division among the church.

Paul said, "4 For while one saith, I am of Paul; and another, I am of Apollos; are ye not carnal? 5 Who then is Paul, and who is Apollos, but ministers by whom ye believed, even as the Lord gave to every man? 6 I have planted, Apollos watered; but God gave the increase. 7 So then neither is he that planteth any thing, neither he that watereth; but God that giveth the increase" 1 Cor 3:4-7.

Paul explained to the church: That they all are workers together with God, showing them that there is no need for division.

Paul said, "8 Now he that planteth and he that watereth are one: and every man shall receive his own reward according to his own labour. 9 For we are labourers together with God: ye are God's husbandry, ye are God's building. 10 According to the grace of God which is given unto me, as a wise masterbuilder, I have laid the foundation, and another buildeth thereon. But let every man take heed how he buildeth thereupon. 11 For other foundation can no man lay than that is laid, which is Jesus Christ" 1 Cor 3:8-11.

I Have Provided A List Of Some Of The Most Popular Denominations Founded By Men And Women In America.

The Roman Catholic Denomination: Was Founded By "Boniface The 3rd" In 606 A.D.

The Baptist Denomination: Founded By "Roger Williams" In 1639 In America, Soon After He Left It To Become A Seeker Opposed All Sects And Creeds. He Denounced The Baptist.

The Methodist Denomination: Founded By "John Wesley" In 1739.

The Seven Day Adventist Denomination: Founded By "William Miller" In 1830.

The Jehovah's Witness Denomination: Founded By "Charles T. Russell" In 1872.

The Church Of God In Christ Denomination: Founded By Two Baptist Preachers, "Charles Price Jones" And "Charles H. Mason" In Memphis Tennessee In 1897.

The Pentecostal Church Inc Denomination: Found In 1899 In Topeka, Kansas. The Pentecostal Assembly Of Jesus Christ, Inc. Became So Closely Associated In Doctrine And Fellowship That In 1944 They Were United Into What Is Known As "The United Pentecostal Church".

The Church Of Christ Scientist Denomination: Founded By "Mary Baker Eddy" In New England In 1879.

The Black Hebrew Israelite Denomination: Believed To Have Been Founded By Some Black Hispanics, And Some Black African Americans; It Is Believed That Is Was Founded In The Late 1800s.

Even thou the Bible teach that denominationalism is against God; look at all of the people that are divided religiously; knowing that those denominations do not have salvation in them.

Peter said, "10 Be it known unto you all, and to all the people of Israel, that by the name of Jesus Christ of Nazareth, whom ye crucified, whom God raised from the dead, even by him doth this man stand here before you whole. 11 this is the stone which was set at nought of you builders, which is become the head of the corner. 12 neither is there salvation in any other:

for there is none other name under heaven given among men, whereby we must be saved" Acts 4:10-12.

The denominational preachers maybe offended like the Pharisees were: Let us hear what Jesus said about them!

The Bible said, "12 Then came his disciples, and said unto him, knowest thou that the pharisees were offended, after they heard this saying? 13 but he answered and said, every plant, which my heavenly father hath not planted, shall be rooted up. 14 let them alone: they be blind leaders of the blind. and if the blind lead the blind, both shall fall into the ditch" Matt 15:12-14.

Baptism: Makes People New

Spiritual Baptism: Is A Spiritual Burial That Takes Place In Physical Or Natural Water.

Men and Brethren: When people are born into the world and live to the age of accountability knowing right from wrong, at that time they must make a decision to be baptized in water to save their soul or refuse to be baptized and lose their soul.

The Bible said, "4 Nicodemus saith unto him, How can a man be born when he is old? can he enter the second time into his mother's womb, and be born? 5 Jesus answered, Verily, verily, I say unto thee, Except a man be born of water and of the Spirit, he cannot enter into the kingdom of God. 6 That which is born of the flesh is flesh; and that which is born of the Spirit is spirit.

7 Marvel not that I said unto thee, Ye must be born again" John 3:4-7.

According to Jesus: There is no way for a person to be clean from their sins without being Baptized, Immersed, or Submerge in water according to the scriptures!

The Bible said, "18 And Jesus came and spake unto them, saying, All power is given unto me in heaven and in earth. 19 Go ye therefore, and teach all nations, baptizing them in the name of the Father, and of the Son, and of the Holy Ghost: 20 Teaching them to observe all things whatsoever

I have commanded you: and, lo, I am with you alway, even unto the end of the world. Amen" Matt 28:18-20.

The Bible said, "15 And he said unto them, Go ye into all the world, and preach the gospel to every creature. 16 He that believeth and is baptized shall be saved; but he that believeth not shall be damned" Mark 16:15-16.

Baptism: Is A Spiritual Life Changing Experience; That Transforms People From Their Old Carnal (Sinful) Way Of Life, Into A New Spiritual (Godly) Way Of Life.

Paul said, "1 What shall we say then? Shall we continue in sin, that grace may abound? 2 God forbid. How shall we, that are dead to sin, live any longer therein? 3 Know ye not, that so many of us as were baptized into Jesus Christ were baptized into his death? 4 Therefore we are buried with him by baptism into death: that like as Christ was raised up from the dead by the glory of the Father, even so we also should walk in newness of life. 5 For if we have been planted together in the likeness of his death, we shall be also in the likeness of his resurrection: 6 Knowing this, that our old man is crucified with him, that the body of sin might be destroyed, that henceforth we should not serve sin. 7 For he that is dead is freed from sin" (Romans 6:1-7).

Paul said, "17 Therefore if any man be in Christ, he is a new creature: old things are passed away; behold, all things are become new" 2 Corinthians 5:17.

After people have been baptized into Jesus Christ; they are taught how to remain being a faithful Christian, so that they will not fall back into the snares of the Devil.

Peter said, "15 But let none of you suffer as a murderer, or as a thief, or as an evildoer, or as a busybody in other men's matters. 16 Yet if any man suffer as a Christian, let him not be ashamed; but let him glorify God on this behalf" 1 Peter 4:15-16.

The Bible Teaches: That there are 5 things that God requires that all mankind must do to become a Christian.

#1: They must: Hear the word of God.

Jesus said, "44 No man can come to me, except the Father which hath sent me draw him: and I will raise him up at the last day. It is written in the prophets, 45 And they shall be all taught of God. Every man therefore that hath heard, and hath learned of the Father, cometh unto me" John 6:44-45.

#2: They must: Believe that God rose up Christ from the dead.

Paul said, "9 That if thou shalt confess with thy mouth the Lord Jesus, and shalt believe in thine heart that God hath raised him from the dead, thou shalt be saved. 10 For with the heart man believeth unto righteousness; and with the mouth confession is made unto salvation" (Romans 10:9-10).

#3: They must: Repent of their sins.

Peter said, "37 Now when they heard this, they were pricked in their heart, and said unto Peter and to the rest of the apostles, Men and brethren, what shall we do? 38 Then Peter said unto them, Repent, and be baptized every one of you in the name of Jesus Christ for the remission of sins, and ye shall receive the gift of the Holy Ghost" Acts 2:37-38.

#4: They must: Confess that they believe that Jesus Christ is the Son of God.

Jesus said, "32 Whosoever therefore shall confess me before men, him will I confess also before my Father which is in heaven. 33 But whosoever shall deny me before men, him will I also deny before my Father which is in heaven" Matthew 10:32-33.

#5: They must: Be Baptized for the remission of their sins.

The Bible said, "36 And as they went on their way, they came unto a certain water: and the eunuch said, See, here is water; what doth hinder me to be baptized? 37 And Philip said, If thou believest with all thine heart, thou mayest. And he answered and said, I believe that Jesus Christ is the Son of God. 38 And he commanded the chariot to stand still: and they went down both into the water, both Philip and the eunuch; and he baptized him. 39 And when they were come up out of the water, the Spirit of the Lord caught away Philip, that the eunuch saw him no more: and he went on his way rejoicing" Acts 8:36-39.

Baptism is the evident that people have been taught and understand that they have laid aside all of their evil ways and has been forgiven for them, they also realize that they have become as a newborn infant, hungry for the word of God that they may grow thereby.

The Devil has many false teachers who are teaching people that pouring or sprinkling water on infants will save them from their sins, this false teaching is truly the doctrines of Devils, because infants cannot do the things that God require that all mankind must do to become Christians. Infants cannot Hear the word of God, they cannot Believe the word of God, they do not have any sin to Repent of, they cannot Confess their faith in Christ, they cannot be Baptized on their own ability as God require that all mankind must do to wash away their sins.

The Bible said, "1 At the same time came the disciples unto Jesus, saying, Who is the greatest in the kingdom of heaven? 2 And Jesus called a little child unto him, and set him in the midst of them, 3 And said, Verily I say unto you, Except ye be converted, and become as little children, ye shall not enter into the kingdom of heaven. 4 Whosoever therefore shall humble himself as this little child, the same is greatest in the kingdom of heaven" Matt 18:1-4.

Pouring Or Sprinkling Water On Infants Or On Anyone Else Will Not Save Them From Their Sins.

The Devil: Knows that when mankind is baptized into Jesus Christ; they become new creatures: which means they are no longer under his devilish power; and their old sinful ways of life are passed away; and all things are become new. The Devil wants all mankind both young and old to die in their sin; so that they will spend eternity with him in Hell.

Men and Brethren: Regardless to what the Devil or what anyone else has to say, being baptized in water still washes away sin, even in these days.

Peter said, "20 Which sometime were disobedient, when once the longsuffering of God waited in the days of Noah, while the ark was a preparing, wherein few, that is, eight souls were saved by water. 21 The like figure whereunto even baptism doth also now save us (not the putting away of the filth of the flesh, but the answer of a good conscience toward God,) by the resurrection of Jesus Christ" 1 Peter 3:20-21.

The Bible Teaches: All Christians Must Have A Desire To Grow.

Peter said, "1 Wherefore laying aside all malice, and all guile, and hypocrisies, and envies, and all evil speakings, 2 As newborn babes, desire the sincere milk of the word, that ye may grow thereby: 3 If so be ye have tasted that the Lord is gracious" 1 Peter 2:1-3.

Bishops: Are Necessary In The Churches Of Christ In These Days

During the days of the Apostles: Bishops were the men that were usually in charge of the finances or money among the Apostles.

During the days of the Apostles: Judas worked as a Bishop among the Apostles.

The Bible said, "1 Then Jesus six days before the passover came to Bethany, where Lazarus was which had been dead, whom he raised from the dead. 2 There they made him a supper; and Martha served: but Lazarus was one of them that sat at the table with him. 3 Then took Mary a pound of ointment of spikenard, very costly, and anointed the feet of Jesus, and wiped his feet with her hair: and the house was filled with the odour of the ointment" John 12:1-3.

The Bible said, "4 Then saith one of his disciples, Judas Iscariot, Simon's son, which should betray him, 5 Why was not this ointment sold for three hundred pence, and given to the poor? 6 This he said, not that he cared for the poor; but because he was a thief, and had the bag, and bare what was put therein" John 12:4-6.

The Bible said, "3 Then Judas, which had betrayed him, when he saw that he was condemned, repented himself, and brought again the thirty pieces of silver to the chief priests and elders, 4 Saying, I have sinned in that I have betrayed the innocent blood. And they said, What is that to us? see thou to that. 5 And he cast down the pieces of silver in the temple, and departed, and went and hanged himself" Matt 27:3-5.

After Judas died: The Holy Ghost commanded the Apostles to choose another person to take his position as an Apostle and as a Bishop!

The Bible said, "15 And in those days peter stood up in the midst of the disciples, and said, (the number of names together were about an hundred and twenty,) 16 men and brethren, this scripture must needs have been fulfilled, which the holy ghost by the mouth of David spoke before concerning Judas, which was guide to them that took Jesus. 20 for it is written in the book of psalms, let his habitation be desolate, and let no man dwell therein: and his bishopric let another take" Acts 1:15-16, 20.

The Bible said, "23 And they appointed two, Joseph called Barabbas, who was surnamed Justus, and Matthias. 24 and they prayed, and said, thou, lord, which knowest the hearts of all men, shew whether of these two thou hast chosen, 25 that he may take part of this ministry and apostleship, from which Judas by transgression fell, that he might go to his own place.

26 and they gave forth their lots; and the lot fell upon Matthias; and he was numbered with the eleven apostles" Acts 1:23-26.

Knowing that this is the way that God wanted things to be; proves that Bishops are necessary in the churches.

According To Paul: Before a man can work in the office of a bishop: he must have 17 qualifications proven before he can work in that office.

Paul said, "1 This is a true saying, if a man desire the office of a bishop, he desireth a good work. 2 a bishop then must be blameless, the husband of one wife, vigilant, sober, of good behaviour, given to hospitality, apt to teach; 3 not given to wine, no striker, not greedy of filthy lucre; but patient, not a brawler, not covetous; 4 one that ruleth well his own house, having his children in subjection with all gravity; 5 (for if a man know not how to rule his own house, how shall he take care of the church of god?) 6 not a novice, lest being lifted up with pride he fall into the condemnation of the devil. 7 moreover he must have a good report of them which are without; lest he fall into reproach and the snare of the devil" 1 Tim 3:1-7.

Paul left Titus in Crete; on a Twofold Mission: Titus First Mission Was To Set In Place The Office Of Bishops: Paul Gave Titus 17 Qualifications That A Man Must Have Proven Before He Can Work In That Office.

Titus Second Mission: Was To Ordain Elders In Every City As Paul Has Appointed Him.

Paul said, "5 For this cause left I thee in Crete, that thou shouldest set in order the things that are wanting, and ordain elders in every city, as I had appointed thee: 6 if any be blameless, the husband of one wife, having faithful children not accused of riot or unruly. 7 for a bishop must be blameless, as the steward of god; not selfwilled, not soon angry, not given to wine, no striker, not given to filthy lucre; 8 but a lover of hospitality, a lover of good men, sober, just, holy, temperate; 9 holding fast the faithful word as he hath been taught, that he may be able by sound doctrine both to exhort and to convince the gainsayers" Titus 1:5-9.

It is very important for the entire world to understand that when Paul talk to Timothy and to Titus about the men that work in the office of a Bishop; Paul said that they must have certain Qualifications; and they must be proven before they can work in that office.

Paul said, "5 Prove all things; hold fast that which is good" 1 Thess 5:21.

The Holy Ghost: Does Not Ordained Elders In The Churches Of Christ Since The Perfect Law Of Liberty Have Come

During the days of the Apostles: the Apostles and Titus ordained the elders of the church by the Supernatural power of the Holy Ghost; which gave them the ability to preach the word of God without them having a written Bible; and those men was presently the overseers of their flocks.

I am writing this epistle: Because there are many false preachers and deceivers, who are teaching things that is contrary to the doctrine of Christ concerning the ordaining of elders in the churches of Christ.

When the church was in its infant state; God put grown men in it to govern it; until the perfect law of liberty come, which is the complete written word of God: the Bible.

Paul said, "18 But now hath God set the members every one of them in the body, as it hath pleased him. 28And God hath set some in the church, first Apostles, secondarily Prophets, thirdly Teachers, after that miracles, then gifts of healings, helps, governments, diversities of tongues" 1 Cor 12:18, 28.

On the day of Pentecost: There were about three thousand people that were baptized into the church; and there were only 12 apostles to teach the people, so then after Pentecost; the Apostle's started ordaining the elders of the church; through the power of the Holy Ghost to help them to preach the word of God.

Paul ordained the elders of the church from Ephesus through the power of the Holy Ghost to preach the word of God.

The Bible said, "17 And from Miletus he sent to Ephesus, and called the elders of the church. 28 take heed therefore unto yourselves, and to all the flock, over the which the Holy Ghost hath made you overseers, to feed the church of God, which he hath purchased with his own blood" Acts 20:17, 28.

It is important to keep in mind that Paul told those elders of the church from Ephesus that grievous wolves was going to entered into the churches through them!

Paul said, "29 For I know this, that after my departing shall grievous wolves enter in among you, not sparing the flock. 30 Also of your own selves shall men arise, speaking perverse things, to draw away disciples after them" Acts 20:29-30

Peter ordained the elders of the church that met with him through the power of the Holy Ghost; to preach the word of God.

Peter said, "1 The elders which are among you i exhort, who am also an elder, and a witness of the sufferings of Christ, and also a partaker of the glory that shall be revealed: 2 feed the flock of God which is among you, taking the oversight thereof, not by constraint, but willingly; not for filthy lucre, but of a ready mind; 3 neither as being lords over god's heritage, but being ensamples to the flock" 1 peter 5:1-3.

When John sealed the epistle of the revelation of Jesus Christ, at that time the perfect law of liberty was complete. The angel told John to send it to the seven churches which are in Asia: and at that time all of the churches of Christ had the complete written word of God.

The Bible said, "1 The Revelation of Jesus Christ, which God gave unto him, to show unto his servants things which must shortly come to pass; and he sent and signified it by his angel unto his servant John: 3 Blessed is he that readeth, and they that hear the words of this prophecy, and keep those things which are written therein: for the time is at hand. 4 John to the seven churches which are in Asia: Grace be unto you, and peace, from him which is, and which was, and which is to come; and from the seven Spirits which are before his throne; 10 I was in the Spirit on the Lord's day, and heard behind me a great voice, as of a trumpet, 11 Saying, I am Alpha and Omega, the first and the last: and, What thou seest, write in a book, and send it unto the seven churches which are in Asia; unto Ephesus, and unto Smyrna, and unto Pergamos, and unto Thyatira, and unto Sardis, and unto Philadelphia, and unto Laodicea" Rev 1:1, 3-4, 10-11.

In these days: There are many false and disobedient Gospel Preachers: Who are bogusly ordaining men who are not presently the overseers of their flocks, and those gospel preachers do not have the authoritative power of the Holy Ghost to ordain those men. All of those gospel preachers and those false elders will receive to themselves the recompense of their error if they do not repent.

It is very important for all Bible believing people to understand that when the last Apostle died, the performing of miracles ceased, the lying on of hands and imparting spiritual gifts to others ceased, and the ability to ordain elders of the church by the Authoritative Power of the Holy Ghost ceased.

Paul explained to the church in Corinth, that the things that they did in the church before the perfect law of liberty came, was done in part: And he told them that when the perfect law of Liberty come, those things will cease.

Paul said, "8 Charity never faileth: but whether there be prophecies, they shall fail; whether there be tongues, they shall cease; whether there be knowledge, it shall vanish away. 9 For we know in part, and we prophesy in part. 10 But when that which is perfect is come, then that which is in part shall be done away" 1 Corinthians 13:8-10.

Men and Brethren: Paul used a perfect metaphor to prove that when the church of Christ drew from its infant state to completion, that there were some positions that was no longer needed.

Paul said, "11 When I was a child, I spake as a child, I understood as a child, I thought as a child: but when I became a man, I put away childish things. 12 For now we see through a glass, darkly; but then face to face: now I know in part; but then shall I know even as also I am known" 1 Cor 13:11-12.

The Overseers Of The Churches Of Christ: In These Last Days

My reason for writing this lesson is: Because the Devil has persuaded his false gospel preachers to ignore the office of a Bishop, because his devilish intension was to stop that good work of the church that was done in that office.

And I am also writing this lesson: Because I want the people to know that the devil is causing many Christians and non Christians to go down that Broadway that lead to destruction, simply because they are been bamboozled and misled by many false gospel preachers and others who are teaching that the office of a Bishop have ceased to be.

Paul said, "1 This is a true saying, If a man desire the office of a bishop, he desireth a good work" 1 Tim 3:1.

We need to understand that when the church of Christ started, God set three groups of men in it; and those men were; first the apostles, and secondarily the prophets, and thirdly teachers, and those men were to govern and to oversee the church until the perfect law of liberty comes.

Paul said, "28 And God hath set some in the church, first apostles, secondarily prophets, thirdly teachers, after that miracles, then gifts of healings, helps, governments, diversities of tongues" 1 Cor 12:28.

Paul said, "8 charity never faileth: but whether there be prophecies, they shall fail; whether there be tongues, they shall cease; whether there be knowledge, it shall vanish away. 9 for we know in part, and we prophesy in part. 10 but when that which is perfect is come, then that which is in part shall be done away" 1 Cor 13:8-10.

Now let us keep in mind, that since the perfect law of liberty has come, and since the Apostles, the Prophets, and the Elders of the church no longer exist, therefore the truth is, that in these last days, gospel preachers are the overseers of the church.

Paul said to the church of Christ in Rome: That a preacher must be sent to preach the gospel of Christ.

Paul said, "13 For whosoever shall call upon the name of the Lord shall be saved.

14 How then shall they call on him in whom they have not believed? and how shall they believe in him of whom they have not heard? and how shall they hear without a preacher?

15 And how shall they preach, except they be sent? as it is written, How beautiful are the feet of them that preach the gospel of peace, and bring glad tidings of good things" Romans 10:13-15.

The Hebrews writer told the church to obey them that have the rule of them; the Hebrews writer was talking about gospel preachers.

The Bible said, "17 Obey them that have the rule over you, and submit yourselves: for they watch for your souls, as they that must give account, that they may do it with joy, and not with grief: for that *is* unprofitable for you" Heb 13:17.

Jude wrote to the church of Christ, exhorting the gospel preachers to earnestly contend for the faith.

Jude said, "3 Beloved, when I gave all diligence to write unto you of the common salvation, it was needful for me to write unto you, and exhort you that ye should earnestly contend for the faith which was once delivered unto the saints. 4 For there are certain men crept in unawares, who were before of old ordained to this condemnation, ungodly men, turning the grace of our God into lasciviousness, and denying the only Lord God, and our Lord Jesus Christ" Jude 1:3-4.

The Apostles sent out several men to preach the gospel of Christ and none of those men was Ordain to be the Elders of the Church.

(Timothy) Paul said, "1 I charge thee therefore before God, and the Lord Jesus Christ, who shall judge the quick and the dead at his appearing and his kingdom; 2 Preach the word; be instant in season, out of season; reprove, rebuke, exhort with all longsuffering and doctrine" 2 Tim 4:1-2.

(Titus) Paul said, "4 To Titus, mine own son after the common faith: Grace, mercy, and peace, from God the Father and the Lord Jesus Christ our Saviour. 5 For this cause left I thee in Crete, that thou shouldest set in order the things that are wanting, and ordain elders in every city, as I had appointed thee" Titus 1:4-5.

Paul said, "7 All my state shall **Tychicus** declare unto you, who is a beloved brother, and a faithful **minister** and fellowservant in the Lord: 8 Whom I have sent unto you for the same purpose, that he might know your estate, and comfort your hearts; 9 With **Onesimus**, a faithful and beloved brother, who is one of you. They shall make known unto you all things which are done here.10 **Aristarchus** my fellowprisoner saluteth you, and **Marcus**, sister's son to Barnabas, (touching whom ye received commandments: if he come unto you, receive him;) 11 And **Jesus**, which is called **Justus**, who are of the circumcision. These only are my fellowworkers unto the **kingdom of God**, which have been a comfort unto me. 12 **Epaphras**, who is one of you, a servant of Christ, saluteth you, always labouring fervently for you in prayers, that ye may stand perfect and complete in all the will of God. 13 For I bear him record, that he hath a great zeal for you, and them that are in Laodicea, and them in Hierapolis" Col 4:7-13.

Brethren; doesn't it seem hypocritical, that some gospel preachers in the churches of Christ teach against the false denominational churches for wearing the titles of the Apostles that no longer exist; And for wearing the titles of the prophets that no longer exist; And they are using men in their congregations that are wearing the titles of the elders of the church that no longer exist?

It is so heart breaking to know that there are so many gospel preachers in the congregations of the churches of Christ who are too stiff necked to teach that the office of a Bishop does exist in the churches of Christ.

Paul said, "51 Ye stiffnecked and uncircumcised in heart and ears, ye do always resist the Holy Ghost: as your fathers did, so do ye" Acts 7:51.

Modern-Day Women: Must Be Governed By The Written Word Of God

I am writing this subject; in hope that all women in the entire world will learn and obey the roll that God have put in place for women to follow; regardless to what Gloria Steinem or anyone else have to say that is contrary to what the Bible, the written word of God said.

Women liberation is the act or process of trying to achieve equal rights and status as male counterpart. In the late 60s and 70s, the women's liberation movement radically altered America perception of the female sex, but sexual liberation was just a small part of the bigger social movement agitating for women's independence and equality, also known as feminism.

When you read the history of Gloria Steinem, women liberation in America, you will learn that the leading feminist base their belief and behavior totally on feminism and social political and economic equality of the sexes the movement organized around that belief.

Long before the women liberation movement came about in America, there were women who had used their liberty to get what they wanted out of men, even though it came with a great cost.

Adam's wife Eve; used her Liberty: Over her husband in the Garden of Eden and it caused them both to be put out of the garden forever, because of her sin.

The Bible said, "6 And when the woman saw that the tree was good for food, and that it was pleasant to the eyes, and a tree to be desired to make one wise, she took of the fruit thereof, and did eat, and gave also unto her husband with her; and he did eat. 17 And unto Adam he said, Because thou hast hearkened unto the voice of thy wife, and hast eaten of the tree, of which I commanded thee, saying, Thou shalt not eat of it: cursed is the ground for thy sake; in sorrow shalt thou eat of it all the days of thy life; 23 Therefore the LORD God sent him forth from the garden of Eden, to till the ground from whence he was taken" Gen 3:6, 17, 23.

Abram's wife Sarai; used her Liberty: Over her husband, and it caused them both to sin.

The Bible said, "3 And Sarai Abram's wife took Hagar her maid the Egyptian, after Abram had dwelt ten years in the land of Canaan, and gave her to her husband Abram to be his wife. 4 And he went in unto Hagar, and she conceived: and when she saw that she had conceived, her mistress was despised in her eyes. 5 And Sarai said unto Abram, My wrong be upon thee: I have given my maid into thy bosom; and when she saw that she had conceived, I was despised in her eyes: the LORD judge between me and thee" Gen 16:3-5.

Samson's wife Delilah; used her Liberty: Over her husband and it cause him to lose his life.

The Bible said, "16 And it came to pass, when she pressed him daily with her words, and urged him, so that his soul was vexed unto death; 17 That he told her all his heart, and said unto her, There hath not come a razor upon mine head; for I have been a Nazarite unto God from my mother's womb: if I be shaven, then my strength will go from me, and I shall become weak, and be like any other man. 18 And when Delilah saw that he had told her all his heart, she sent and called for the lords of the Philistines, saying, Come up this once, for he hath shewed me all his heart. Then the lords of the Philistines came up unto her, and brought money in their hand. 29 And Samson took hold of the two middle pillars upon which the house stood, and on which it was borne up, of the one with his right hand, and of the other with his left. 30 And Samson said, Let me die with the Philistines. And he bowed himself with all his might; and the house fell upon the lords, and upon all the people that were therein. So the dead which he slew at his death were more than they which he slew in his life" Judges 16: 16-18, 29-30.

Jezebel; used her Liberty to teach God's people: Over his will and God caused her to be thrown out of a window and to be eaten by dogs until she was unrecognizable.

The Bible said, "33 And he said, Throw her down. So they threw her down: and some of her blood was sprinkled on the wall, and on the horses: and he trode her under foot. 34 And when he was come in, he did eat and drink, and said, Go, see now this cursed woman, and bury her: for she is a king's daughter. 35 And they went to bury her: but they found no more of her than the skull, and the feet, and the palms of her hands. 36 Wherefore they came again, and told him. And he said, This is the word of the LORD, which he spake by his servant Elijah the Tishbite, saying, In the portion of Jezreel shall dogs eat the flesh of Jezebel: 37 And the carcase of Jezebel shall be as dung upon the face of the field in the portion of Jezreel; so that they shall not say, This is Jezebel" 2 Kings 9:33-37.

The Phrase Liberty Means: Freedom; Independence; Authority; Autonomy; Permission; and Liberation.

The Bible teaches that God gave the preeminence over the churches of Christ to gospel preachers; who shall teach the entire world to keep the ordinances of God.

Paul said, "1 Be ye followers of me, even as I also am of Christ. 2 Now I praise you, brethren, that ye remember me in all things, and keep the ordinances, as I delivered them to you. 3 But I would have you know, that the head of every man is Christ; and the head of the woman is the man; and the head of Christ is God" 1 Cor 11:1-3.

The major problem with women Liberation in the churches of Christ is: Because there are so many false gospel preachers who have given their wives and other women the authority to use their congregation to preach or to teach to other women, and there is absolutely no place in the doctrine of Christ or in the apostles doctrine where the God of heaven; or his son, Jesus Christ; or the Holy Ghost has ever given the authority to any gospel preacher to give women the authority to teach or to preach the word of God in the church building by no means whatsoever: And those gospel preachers who are allowing women to do so are in total violation of the doctrine of Christ.

If all gospel preachers would take the time and remember what Paul said to the church of Christ in Roman 15:4-6; then we all would be doing the will of God and he would be will pleased with all of us.

Paul said, "4 For whatsoever things were written aforetime were written for our learning, that we through patience and comfort of the scriptures might have hope. 5 Now the God of patience and consolation grant you to be likeminded one toward another according to Christ Jesus: 6 That ye may with one mind and one mouth glorify God, even the Father of our Lord Jesus Christ" Romans 15:4-6.

All Gospel Preachers Need To Remember: That God Told Eve, That Her Desire Shall Be To Her Husband, And He Shall Rule Over Her.

The Bible said, "16 Unto the woman he said, I will greatly multiply thy sorrow and thy conception; in sorrow thou shalt bring forth children; and thy desire shall be to thy husband, and he shall rule over thee" Genesis 3:16.

All Gospel Preachers Need To Remember: What Paul Told Timothy; About Adam And Eve.

Paul said, "13 For Adam was first formed, then Eve. 14 And Adam was not deceived, but the woman being deceived was in the transgression" 1 Tim 2:13-14.

All Gospel Preachers Need To Remember: What Paul Told Timothy; About Allowing Women To Teach.

Paul said, "12 But I suffer not a woman to teach, nor to usurp authority over the man, but to be in silence. 1 Tim 2:12.

All Gospel Preachers Need To Remember: That God Reprimanded The Angel Of The Church In Thyatira For Giving Jezebel; The Permission To Teach His People.

The Bible said, "20 Notwithstanding I have a few things against thee, because thou sufferest that woman Jezebel, which calleth herself a prophetess, to teach and to seduce my servants to commit fornication, and to eat things sacrificed unto idols. 21 And I gave her space to repent of her fornication; and she repented not." Revelation 2:20-21.

All Gospel Preachers Need To Remember: That Peter Taught The Women In The Church Of Christ Concerning The Mannerisms That Holy Women Or Christians Women Should Live By.

Peter said, "5 For after this manner in the old time the holy women also, who trusted in God, adorned themselves, being in subjection unto their own husbands: 6 Even as Sara obeyed Abraham, calling him lord: whose daughters ye are, as long as ye do well, and are not afraid with any amazement" 1 Peter 3:5-6.

There are many false gospel preachers in the churches of Christ, also in the religious denominational world today, that are allowing women who call themselves Women of Empowerment: Reverend: Preacher: Apostle: and Evangelist to preach the word of God; a thing that have never been permissible by God, and if these men and women do not stop violating the word of God and repent of their heinous behavior and turn or return to God; so that he will forgive them of their sins, then truly they will spend eternity in everlasting punishment.

It does not matter who we are or what our positions are in life: All mankind is governed by the scripture; the written word of God: And we all must obey them to be saved.

Paul said, "16 All scripture is given by inspiration of God, and is profitable for doctrine, for reproof, for correction, for instruction in righteousness: 17 That the man of God may be perfect, throughly furnished unto all good works" 2 Tim 3:16-17.

Even though the world that we are living in; have become so chaotic; and it is getting worse day by day; yet the God of heaven is still saying that the modern-day women must obey his word the same as everyone else; that want to be saved.

The Bible said, "7 Let the wicked forsake his way, and the unrighteous man his thoughts: and let him return unto the LORD, and he will have mercy upon him; and to our God, for he will abundantly pardon. 8 For my thoughts are not your thoughts, neither are your ways my ways, saith the LORD. 9 For as the heavens are higher than the earth, so are my ways higher than your ways, and my thoughts than your thoughts" Isaiah 55:7-9.

The Truth: Concerning Widows And Widows Indeed In the Churches Of Christ

Widows Are Women Whose Husbands Are Dead; And They Did Not Remarry.

In Asia: when the church of Christ was multiplying rapidly; some of the people thought that their widows were being neglected or overlooked; doing their daily distribution of the food that they were giving to the widows: The Apostles knew that God commanded that his people are to be taken care of; so they told the people to choose some men that they shall appoint over that business.

The Bible said, "1 And in those days, when the number of the disciples was multiplied, there arose a murmuring of the Grecians against the Hebrews, because their widows were neglected in the daily ministration. 2 Then the twelve called the multitude of the disciples unto them, and said, It is not reason that we should leave the word of God, and serve tables. 3 Wherefore, brethren, look ye out among you seven men of honest report, full of the Holy Ghost and wisdom, whom we may appoint over this business" Acts 6:1-3.

The Bible said, "10 Bring ye all the tithes into the storehouse, that there may be meat in mine house, and prove me now herewith, saith the LORD of hosts, if I will not open you the windows of heaven, and pour you out a blessing, that there shall not be room enough to receive it" Mal 3:10.

Paul had a conversation with Timothy: Concerning the congregations of the churches of Christ that have widows: Paul explained to Timothy in step-by-step details on how each congregation are required to take care of their widows: Paul further explained to Timothy; the difference between widows and widows indeed.

Paul also explained to Timothy: That the congregations of the churches of Christ that have widows, who are not widows indeed; are not required to support them financially, The family of these widows are required to support them financially.

Paul said, "3 Honour widows that are widows indeed. 4 But if any widow have children or nephews, let them learn first to shew piety at home, and to requite their parents: for that is good and acceptable before God. 16 If any man or woman that believeth have widows, let them relieve them, and let not the church be charged; that it may relieve them that are widows indeed" 1 Tim 5:3-4, 16.

Naomi Is A Profound Example Of A Widow: Who Was Not A Widow Indeed.

The Bible said, "11 And Naomi said, Turn again, my daughters: why will ye go with me? are there yet any more sons in my womb, that they may be your husbands? 16 And Ruth said, Intreat me not to leave thee, or to return from following after thee: for whither thou goest, I will go; and where thou lodgest, I will lodge: thy people shall be my people, and thy God my God: 19 So they two went until they came to Bethlehem. And it came to pass, when they were come to Bethlehem, that all the city was moved about them, and they said, Is this Naomi? 20 And she said unto them, Call me not Naomi, call me Mara: for the Almighty hath dealt very bitterly with me. 21 I went out full, and the LORD hath brought me home again empty: why then call ye me Naomi, seeing the LORD hath testified against me, and the Almighty hath afflicted me? 22 So Naomi returned, and Ruth the Moabitess, her daughter in law, with her, which returned out of the country of Moab: and they came to Bethlehem in the beginning of barley harvest" Ruth 1:11, 16, 19-22.

Paul gave Timothy 12 Qualifications that widows indeed must have in order for a congregation to support them financially, and if those qualifications are not met; then the congregation is not required to support them financially.

Paul said, "5 Now she that is a widow indeed, and desolate, trusteth in God, and continueth in supplications and prayers night and day. 7 And these things give in charge, that they may be blameless. 9 let not a widow be taken into the number under threescore years old, having been the wife of one man.10 Well reported of for good works; if she have brought up children, if she have lodged strangers, if she have washed the saints' feet, if she have relieved the afflicted, if she have diligently followed every good work" 1 Tim 5:5, 7, 9-10.

Even though Paul taught Timothy all of the fundamentals things concerning widows in the churches of Christ; there are still congregations in the churches of Christ that are financially supporting widows of deceased ministers; and those widows are not widows indeed; and there are other widows in those same congregations who are not widows indeed and they are not receiving financial support from those congregations: Brethren; the congregations that are financially supporting some widows who are not widows indeed; and are not financially supporting all other widows who are not widows indeed; are showing partiality; and to be partial is sin according to the scriptures.

Paul said, "20 Them that sin rebuke before all, that others also may fear. 21 I charge thee before God, and the Lord Jesus Christ, and the elect angels, that thou observe these things without preferring one before another, doing nothing by partiality" 1 Tim 5:20-21.

Have you ever known any widows indeed and their congregation financially supports those widows?

Paul said, "10 Now I beseech you, brethren, by the name of our Lord Jesus Christ, that ye all speak the same thing, and that there be no divisions among you; but that ye be perfectly joined together in the same mind and in the same judgment" 1 Cor 1:10.

Men and Brethren: Can't you see the dilemma or the predicament that many congregations of the churches of Christ have allow the Devil to put them in, and he is causing them to go down that Broadway that leads to destruction.

Jesus said, "13 Enter ye in at the strait gate: for wide is the gate, and broad is the way, that leadeth to destruction, and many there be which go in there at: 14 Because strait is the gate, and narrow is the way, which leadeth unto life, and few there be that find it" Matt 7:13-14.

The Truth: Concerning Funerals

The Purpose Of Funerals: Is To Bury Dead People

Funerals: Is a time to weep with, and to comfort the family, and friends of the deceased person.

Comfort: Is to soothe both the believers and the unbeliever's grief. It is to ease the physical feeling of death. It is to help the unbelievers to believe in God and in Jesus Christ, so that they can turn to them for the remission of their sins.

Men and Brethren: I deemed it necessary to write this subject: Concerning Funerals, so that the entire world can get the full understanding of them: Because there are so many false teachers of the Devil, that are teaching things at funerals that is causing many people of God to misunderstand the truth concerning dead people.

The Devil has caused and is causing many religious and non-religious people to totally disregard the purpose of funerals; and he has caused them to believe that they are having a Home Going Celebration for the dead person simply because; he has cause them to believe that the dead person went directly, or immediately to heaven after they died: Which is another one of his lies.

In order for a gospel preacher or whosoever is officiating, a funeral ceremony to comfort the family of a deceased person, we all must tell the people the truth concerning death from the Bible point of view. We must tell the people that when a person die, they do not go directly or immediately to heaven.

James and Solomon describe death as when the spirit separate from the body.

James said, "26 For as the body without the spirit is dead, so faith without works is dead also" James 2:26.

Solomon said, "10 Whatsoever thy hand findeth to do, do *it* with thy might; for *there is* no work, nor device, nor knowledge, nor wisdom, in the grave, whither thou goest" Eccl 9:10.

Solomon said, "5 Also when they shall be afraid of that which is high, and fears shall be in the way, and the almond tree shall flourish, and the grasshopper shall be a burden, and desire shall fail: because man goeth to his long home, and the mourners go about the streets" Eccl 12:5:

The long home where the dead people souls will go to after they die: To the servants of righteousness; it will go to Abraham's Bosom: To the servants of sin; it will go to hell.

Paul said, "16 Know ye not, that to whom ye yield yourselves to obey, his servants ye are to whom ye obey; whether of sin unto death, or of obedience unto righteousness?" Romans 6:16.

The Bible said, "21 Then said Jesus again unto them, I go my way, and ye shall seek me, and shall die in your sins: whither I go, ye cannot come. 24 I said therefore unto you, that ye shall die in your sins: for if ye believe not that I am he, ye shall die in your sins" John 8:21, 24.

According to the Bible; when a person dies, the spirit goes back to God: And the body returns unto the earth.

Solomon said, "7 Then shall the dust return to the earth as it was: and the spirit shall return unto God who gave it" Eccl 12:7.

Men and Brethren: It is time for all gospel preachers or whosoever is officiating a funeral ceremony: To stop following the customs and the traditions of the heathen, during funeral ceremonies.

Jeremiah said, "1 Hear ye the word which the lord speaketh unto you, o house of Israel: 2 thus saith the lord, learn not the way of the heathen, and be not dismayed at the signs of heaven; for the heathen are dismayed at them" Jer 10:1-2.

Please hear me: I am not trying to be harsh or insensitive: Yet the truth is; that Jesus did not take his friend Lazarus or any other saint directly or immediately to heaven after they died.

Furthermore: Jesus did not call his dead friend, Lazarus from heaven, Jesus called him from the grave; and when Christ come again to receive his church into heaven; he will call those who died in the Lord first; and then he will call the living saints to meet them in the air.

Paul said, "16 For the lord himself shall descend from heaven with a shout, with the voice of the archangel, and with the trump of god: and the dead in Christ shall rise first: 17 then we which are alive and remain shall be caught up together with them in the clouds, to meet the lord in the air: and so shall we ever be with the lord. 18 wherefore comfort one another with these words" 1 Thess 4:16-18.

My prayers to God is: That the Entire World will learn the truth about dead people, and stop believing, and being misled by the lies, that are being told from the Devil that dead people go directly, or immediately to heaven after they die. You see the Devil knows that if he can cause people to believe his lies until they die; that he will surely cause their souls to spend eternity with him in hell.

The Truth: About Holidays

Holiday: A day on which custom or the law dictates a halting of general business activity to commemorate or celebrate a particular event.

Holidays are times when people, friends, and families comes together to celebrate particular days with ceremonies, festivity, and rejoicing.

Paul said, "10 Ye observe days, and months, and times, and years. 11 I am afraid of you, lest I have bestowed upon you labour in vain" Gal 4:10-11.

There are several holidays that are celebrated in the world.

Days such as Birthdays, Christmas Day, Easter Sunday, Mother's Day, Father's Day, Anniversary Day, Veteran Day, St. Valentine's Day, Labor Day, Thanksgiving Day and Personal Days.

According to the scripture; Christ birth was a religious or Holy Birth.

The Bible said, "1 Now when Jesus was born in Bethlehem of Judaea in the days of Herod the king, behold, there came wise men from the east to Jerusalem, 2 saying, where is he that is born king of the Jews? for we have seen his star in the east, and are come to worship him. 11 and when they were come into the house, they saw the young child with Mary his mother, and fell down, and worshipped him: and when they had opened their treasures, they presented unto him gifts; gold, and frankincense, and myrrh" Matthew 2:1-2, 11.

The Heathen; Celebrate a holiday that they call Christmas, and it is represented as a holy feast; commemorating the birth of Jesus. And usually they represent it by decorating what they call a Christmas tree.

Jeremiah said, "2 Thus saith the lord, learn not the way of the heathen, and be not dismayed at the signs of heaven; for the heathen are dismayed at them. 3 for the customs of the people are vain: for one cutteth a tree out of the forest, the work of the hands of the workman, with the axe. 4 they deck it with silver and with gold; they fasten it with nails and with hammers, that it move not" Jeremiah 10:2-4.

There are several holidays that fall on the Lord's Day; and many people will not worship God on those particular Lord's Day; instead they celebrate it with their family and friends.

Jesus Said, "37 He that loveth father or mother more than me is not worthy of me: and he that loveth son or daughter more than me is not worthy of me" Matt 10:37.

Paul said, "1 O Foolish Galatians, Who Hath Bewitched You, That Ye Should Not Obey The Truth, Before Whose Eyes Jesus Christ Hath Been Evidently Set Forth, Crucified Among You" Galatians 3:1.

The Truth: About Christmas

Christmas season: Is a time when many people start preparing for their family and friends to come together to have a feast to commemorate and to celebrate the birth of Jesus Christ.

The Bible said, "1 Now when Jesus was born in Bethlehem of Judaea in the days of Herod the king, behold, there came wise men from the east to Jerusalem, 11 and when they were come into the house, they saw the young child with Mary his mother, and fell down, and worshipped him: and when they had opened their treasures, they presented unto him gifts; gold, and frankincense, and myrrh" Matthew 2:1, 11.

In America, people celebrate the traditional anniversary of the birth of Jesus Christ on the 25th of December, that is the time when family and friends come together to feast; and give gifts to one another, now doesn't it seem kind of odd that Christ never receive any gifts from those who are celebrating and give gifts to one another on his allegedly Birth Day?

Let us not forget what Paul told the church of Christ in Galatia.

Paul said, "10 Ye observe days, and months, and times, and years. 11 I am afraid of you, lest I have bestowed upon you labour in vain" Gal 4:10-11.

Paul said, "1 O foolish Galatians, who hath bewitched you, that ye should not obey the truth, before whose eyes Jesus Christ hath been evidently set forth, crucified among you? 2 This only would I learn of you, Received ye the Spirit by the works of the law, or by the hearing of faith? 3 Are ye so foolish? having begun in the Spirit, are ye now made perfect by the flesh? 4 Have ye suffered so many things in vain? If it be yet in vain. 5 He therefore that ministereth to you the Spirit, and worketh miracles among you, doeth he it by the works of the law, or by the hearing of faith" Gal 3:1-5

The Bible teaches that Sunday is the Lord's Day.

John said, "9 I John, who also am your brother, and companion in tribulation, and in the kingdom and patience of Jesus Christ, was in the isle that is called Patmos, for the word of God, and for the testimony of Jesus Christ. 10 I was in the Spirit on the Lord's day, and heard behind me a great voice, as of a trumpet" Rev 1:9-10.

There are some pagan holidays and personal days that fall on Sunday, the Lord's Day, days such as Christmas Day, Easter Sunday, Mother's Day, Father's Day, Anniversary Days, Birth Days, Veteran Days, Valentine's Day, and many Christians forsake the worship of God in order to honor their family and friends on those days which are all vanity in the sight of God.

The Bible said, "5 And thou shalt love the lord thy God with all thine heart, and with all thy soul, and with all thy might. 6 and these words, which I command thee this day, shall be in thine heart" Deut 6:5-6:

Christ said, "37 He that loveth father or mother more than me is not worthy of me: and he that loveth son or daughter more than me is not worthy of me" Matt 10:37.

During the so-call Christmas season: Many people decorate their homes with stringers of flashing lights so that "Santa Claus" will know to stop there; eat a cookie; and to leave some gifts.

The Devil: Is using every damnable evil weapon that he has in his arsenal for his false apostles, his false preachers, and his false teachers to use to destroy the people of God.

Peter said, "1 But there were false prophets also among the people, even as there shall be false teachers among you, who privily shall bring in damnable heresies, even denying the Lord that bought them, and bring upon themselves swift destruction. 2 And many shall follow their pernicious ways; by reason of whom the way of truth shall be evil spoken of" 2 Peter 2:1-2.

When the so-called Christmas season comes, many people, men and women start preparing themselves to represent the spirit of Christmas.

The Devil has in his Arsenal; A Jolly Old Fat Man with a White Beard and a Red Suit, that he call "Santa Claus"; which to the people serve as the personification of the spirit of Christmas. The Devil: Also have many carnal minded men and women who dress themselves in a so-call "Santa Claus Suit"; and they pretend to be representing the spirit of Christmas.

Paul said, "5 For they that are after the flesh do mind the things of the flesh; but they that are after the Spirit the things of the Spirit. 6 For to be carnally minded is death; but to be spiritually minded is life and peace. 7 Because the carnal mind is enmity against God: for it is not subject to the law of God, neither indeed can be. 8 So then they that are in the flesh cannot please God. 9 But ye are not in the flesh, but in the Spirit, if so be that the Spirit of God dwell in you. Now if any man have not the Spirit of Christ, he is none of his" Romans 8:5-9.

Paul said, "17 This I say therefore, and testify in the Lord, that ye henceforth walk not as other Gentiles walk, in the vanity of their mind, 18 Having the understanding darkened, being alienated from the life of God through the ignorance that is in them, because of the blindness of their heart: 19 Who being past feeling have given themselves over unto lasciviousness, to work all uncleanness with greediness. 20 But ye have not so learned Christ; 21 If so be that ye have heard him, and have been taught by him, as the truth is in Jesus: 22 That ye put off concerning the former conversation the old man, which is corrupt according to the deceitful lusts; 23 And be renewed in the spirit of your mind; 24 And that ye put on the new man, which after God is created in righteousness and true holiness. 25 Wherefore putting away lying, speak every man truth with his neighbour: for we are members one of another. 27 Neither give place to the devil" Eph 4:17-25, 27.

John said, "1 Beloved, believe not every spirit, but try the spirits whether they are of God: because many false prophets are gone out into the world" 1 John 4:1.

The Truth: About Christmas Trees

For centuries many people of God has been following the custom of the heathens, by celebrating what is call Christmas; using trees which the heathens use to worship as their idol gods.

The Bible said, "3 Thou shalt have no other gods before me. 4 thou shalt not make unto thee any graven image, or any likeness of any thing that is in heaven above, or that is in the earth beneath, or that is in the water under the earth: 5 thou shalt not bow down thyself to them, nor serve them: for i the lord thy god am a jealous God, visiting the iniquity of the fathers upon the children unto the third and fourth generation of them that hate me; 6 and shewing mercy unto thousands of them that love me, and keep my commandments" Ex 20:3-6.

Jeremiah said, "1 Hear ye the word which the lord speaketh unto you, o house of Israel: 2 thus saith the lord, learn not the way of the heathen, and be not dismayed at the signs of heaven; for the heathen are dismayed at them. 3 for the customs of the people are vain: for one cutteth a tree out of the forest, the work of the hands of the workman, with the axe. 4 they deck it with silver and with gold; they fasten it with nails and with hammers, that it move not. 5 they are upright as the palm tree, but speak not: they must needs be borne, because they cannot go. Be not afraid of them; for they cannot do evil, neither also is it in them to do good" Jer 10:1-5.

Around the last of November people start setting up their Christmas trees that the heathens worship as their idol gods, they decorate the trees with silver and gold stringers, flashing lights and other type decors, usually they put on top of the trees a replica of an angel, or a replica of a star they call "the Star of David; which represent the place where Jesus Christ was born. And on the 25th of December during their grand celebration, they come together and give gifts to one another saying that "Santa Claus" gave them those gifts, another lie that people tell one another.

Paul said, "23 For as i passed by, and beheld your devotions, I found an altar with this inscription, to the unknown God. Whom therefore ye ignorantly worship, him declare I unto you. 24 God that made the world and all things therein, seeing that he is lord of heaven and earth, dwelled not in temples made with hands; 25 neither is worshipped with men's hands, as though he needed any thing, seeing he giveth to all life, and breath, and all things" Acts 17:23-25.

Paul said, "28 For in him we live, and move, and have our being; as certain also of your own poets have said, for we are also his offspring. 29 forasmuch then as we are the offspring of God, we ought not to think that the godhead is like unto gold, or silver, or stone, graven by art and man's device. 30 and the times of this ignorance god winked at; but now commandeth all men every where to repent" Acts 17:28-30.

God said, "6 My people are destroyed for lack of knowledge: because thou hast rejected knowledge, I will also reject thee, that thou shalt be no priest to me: seeing thou hast forgotten the law of thy God, I will also forget thy children" Hosea 4:6.

You Can Shake It And You Can Make It

The Devil: Can throw anything that he wants to at the people of God, and we can shake it.

John said, "4 Ye are of God, little children, and have overcome them: because greater is he that is in you, than he that is in the world" 1 John 4:4.

Paul said, "13 There hath no temptation taken you but such as is common to man: but God is faithful, who will not suffer you to be tempted above that ye are able; but will with the temptation also make a way to escape, that ye may be able to bear it" 1 Corinthians 10:13.

Shaking the temptations of the Devil: Is similar to wet furry animals: That vigorously shake off the water from their bodies to protect their skin.

The Devil: Put Paul in a very dangerous predicament, but instead of Paul panicking and going into some sort of rage, he calmly walked over to the fire and shook off the beast from his hand.

The Bible said, "3 And when Paul had gathered a bundle of sticks, and laid them on the fire, there came a viper out of the heat, and fastened on his hand. 4 And when the barbarians saw the venomous beast hang on his hand, they said among themselves, No doubt this man is a murderer, whom, though he hath escaped the sea, yet vengeance suffereth not to live. 5 And he shook off the beast into the fire, and felt no harm" Acts 28:3-5.

The world and the churches of Christ need to know: That we can shake off fornication from our bodies.

Paul said, "1 Now concerning the things whereof ye wrote unto me: It is good for a man not to touch a woman. 2 Nevertheless, to avoid fornication, let every man have his own wife, and let every woman have her own husband. 3 Let the husband render unto the wife due benevolence: and likewise also the wife unto the husband" 1 Cor 7:1-3.

Paul said, "1 Be ye therefore followers of God, as dear children; 2 And walk in love, as Christ also hath loved us, and hath given himself for us an offering and a sacrifice to God for a sweetsmelling savour. 3 But fornication, and all uncleanness, or covetousness, let it not be once named among you, as becometh saints" Eph 5:1-3.

Paul said, "13 Meats for the belly, and the belly for meats: but God shall destroy both it and them. Now the body is not for fornication, but for the Lord; and the Lord for the body. 18 Flee fornication. Every sin that a man doeth is without the body; but he that committeth fornication sinneth against his own body. 19 What? know ye not that your body is the temple of the Holy Ghost which is in you, which ye have of God, and ye are not your own? 20 For ye are bought with a price: therefore glorify God in your body, and in your spirit, which are God's" 1 Cor 6:13, 18-20.

The world and the churches of Christ need to know: That we can shake off those dead weights that the Devil has shackled us down with.

The Bible said, "1 Wherefore seeing we also are compassed about with so great a cloud of witnesses, let us lay aside every weight, and the sin which doth so easily beset us, and let us run with patience the race that is set before us, 2 Looking unto Jesus the author and finisher of our faith; who for the joy that was set before him endured the cross, despising the shame, and is set down at the right hand of the throne of God. 3 For consider him that endured such contradiction of sinners against himself, lest ye be wearied and faint in your minds" Heb 12:1-3.

Paul said, "20 But ye have not so learned Christ; 21 If so be that ye have heard him, and have been taught by him, as the truth is in Jesus: 22 That ye put off concerning the former conversation the old man, which is corrupt according to the deceitful lusts; 23 And be renewed in the spirit of your mind; 24 And that ye put on the new man, which after God is created in righteousness and true holiness. 25 Wherefore putting away lying, speak every man truth with his neighbour: for we are members one of another. 26 Be ye angry, and sin not: let not the sun go down upon your wrath: 27 Neither give place to the devil" Eph 4:20-27.

Paul said, "28 Let him that stole steal no more: but rather let him labour, working with his hands the thing which is good, that he may have to give to him that needeth. 29 Let no corrupt communication proceed out of your mouth, but that which is good to the use of edifying, that it may minister grace unto the hearers. 30 And grieve not the holy Spirit of God, whereby ye are sealed unto the day of redemption. 31 Let all bitterness, and wrath, and anger, and clamour, and evil speaking, be put away from you, with all malice: 32 And be ye kind one to another, tenderhearted, forgiving one another, even as God for Christ's sake hath forgiven you" Eph 4:28-32.

James said, "14 But if ye have bitter envying and strife in your hearts, glory not, and lie not against the truth. 15 This wisdom descendeth not from above, but is earthly, sensual, devilish. 16 For where envying and strife is, there is confusion and every evil work" James 3:14-16.

The churches of Christ need to know: That we can shake off the divisions that are among us.

Paul said, "10 Now I beseech you, brethren, by the name of our Lord Jesus Christ, that ye all speak the same thing, and that there be no divisions among you; but that ye be perfectly joined together in the same mind and in the same judgment" 1 Cor 1:10.

Paul said, "33 For God is not the author of confusion, but of peace, as in all churches of the saints. 40 Let all things be done decently and in order" 1 Cor 14:33, 40.

Peter said, "11 If any man speak, let him speak as the oracles of God; if any man minister, let him do it as of the ability which God giveth: that God in all things may be glorified through Jesus Christ, to whom be praise and dominion for ever and ever. Amen" 1 Peter 4:11.

James said, "7 Submit yourselves therefore to God. Resist the devil, and he will flee from you. 8 Draw nigh to God, and he will draw nigh to you. Cleanse your hands, ye sinners; and purify your hearts, ye double minded" James 4:7-8.

God Does Not Speak Verbally: To Men In These Last Days

There are many people who believe that the God of heaven has spoken to them verbally in the New Testament time, even thou the Bible said that God does not speak to people in the New Testament time, or in these last days.

The Bible said, "1 God, who at sundry times and in divers manners spake in time past unto the fathers by the prophets, 2 Hath in these last days spoken unto us by his Son, whom he hath appointed heir of all things, by whom also he made the worlds" Heb 1:1-2.

The world and the churches of Christ need to know: That there are preachers who are lying about the word of God.

God said, "31 Behold, I am against the prophets, saith the LORD, that use their tongues, and say, He saith. 32 Behold, I am against them that prophesy false dreams, saith the LORD, and do tell them, and cause my people to err by their lies, and by their lightness; yet I sent them not, nor commanded them: therefore they shall not profit this people at all, saith the LORD" Jer 23:31-32.

The world and the churches of Christ need to know: That God has never authorized a woman to be a prophet nor a preacher.

The Bible said, "1 And Miriam and Aaron spake against Moses because of the Ethiopian woman whom he had married: for he had married an Ethiopian woman. 2 And they said, Hath the LORD indeed spoken only by Moses? hath he not spoken also by us? And the LORD heard it. 4 And the LORD spake suddenly unto Moses, and unto Aaron, and unto Miriam, Come out ye three unto the tabernacle of the congregation. And they three came out. 5 And the LORD came down in the pillar of the cloud, and stood in the door of the tabernacle, and called Aaron and Miriam: and they both came forth" Num 12:1-2, 4-5.

The Bible said, "6 And he said, Hear now my words: If there be a prophet among you, I the LORD will make myself known unto him in a vision, and will speak unto him in a dream. 7 My servant Moses is not so, who is faithful in all mine house. 8 With him will I speak mouth to mouth, even apparently, and not in dark speeches; and the similitude of the LORD shall he behold: wherefore then were ye not afraid to speak against my servant Moses? 9 And the anger of the LORD was kindled against them; and he departed" Num 12:6-9.

The Bible said, "10 And the cloud departed from off the tabernacle; and, behold, Miriam became leprous, white as snow: and Aaron looked upon Miriam, and, behold, she was leprous. 11 And Aaron said unto Moses, Alas, my lord, I beseech thee, lay not the sin upon us, wherein we have done foolishly, and wherein we have sinned. 12 Let her not be as one dead, of whom the flesh is half consumed when he cometh out of his mother's womb? Num 12:10-12.

The world and the churches of Christ need to know: That God does not speak in secret place on the earth.

God said, "19 I have not spoken in secret, in a dark place of the earth: I said not unto the seed of Jacob, Seek ye me in vain: I the LORD speak righteousness, I declare things that are right" Isaiah 45:19.

Jesus told the high priest that he do not speak in secret.

The Bible said, "19 The high priest then asked Jesus of his disciples, and of his doctrine. 20 Jesus answered him, I spake openly to the world; I ever taught in the synagogue, and in the temple, whither the Jews always resort; and in secret have I said nothing. 21 Why askest thou me? ask them which heard me, what I have said unto them: behold, they know what I said" John 18:19-21.

The world and the churches of Christ need to know: That when Christ was teaching his disciples concerning the New Testament, he did not teach them in secret.

The Bible said, "26 And as they were eating, Jesus took bread, and blessed it, and brake it, and gave it to the disciples, and said, Take, eat; this is my body. 27 And he took the cup, and gave thanks, and gave it to them, saying, Drink ye all of it; 28 For this is my blood of the new testament, which is shed for many for the remission of sins" Matt 26:26-28.

The world and the churches of Christ need to know: That when Christ told his disciples that he was going to build his church, he did not teach them in secret.

The Bible said, "18 And I say also unto thee, That thou art Peter, and upon this rock I will build my church; and the gates of hell shall not prevail against it. 19 And I will give unto thee the keys of the kingdom of heaven: and whatsoever thou shalt bind on earth shall be bound in heaven: and whatsoever thou shalt loose on earth shall be loosed in heaven" Matt 16:18-19.

The Bible said, "1 And after six days Jesus taketh Peter, James, and John his brother, and bringeth them up into an high mountain apart, 2 And was transfigured before them: and his face did shine as the sun, and his raiment was white as the light. 3 And, behold, there appeared unto them Moses and Elias talking with him. 4 Then answered Peter, and said unto Jesus, Lord, it is good for us to be here: if thou wilt, let us make here three tabernacles; one for thee, and one for Moses, and one for Elias" Matt 17:1-4.

Peter said, "17 For he received from God the Father honour and glory, when there came such a voice to him from the excellent glory, This is my beloved Son, in whom I am well pleased. 18 And this voice which came from heaven we heard, when we were with him in the holy mount. 19 We have also a more sure word of prophecy; whereunto ye do well that ye take heed, as unto a light that shineth in a dark place, until the day dawn, and the day star arise in your hearts: 20 Knowing this first, that no prophecy of the scripture is of any private interpretation. 21 For the prophecy came not in old time by the will of man: but holy men of God spake as they were moved by the Holy Ghost" 2 Peter 1:17-21.

What You Are Seeking: Is Seeking You

Seeking Means: That A Person Is Looking For Something Or Someone!

There Are Some People, Who Are Seeking: God.

The Bible said, "29 But if from thence thou shalt seek the LORD thy God, thou shalt find him, if thou seek him with all thy heart and with all thy soul" Deut 4:29.

God said, "17 I love them that love me; and those that seek me early shall find me" Prov 8:17.

The Bible said, "24 God that made the world and all things therein, seeing that he is Lord of heaven and earth, dwelleth not in temples made with hands; 26 And hath made of one blood all nations of men for to dwell on all the face of the earth, and hath determined the times before appointed, and the bounds of their habitation; 27 That they should seek the Lord, if haply they might feel after him, and find him, though he be not far from every one of us: 28 For in him we live, and move, and have our being; as certain also of your own poets have said, For we are also his offspring" Acts 17:24, 26-28.

There Are Some People, Who Are Seeking: To Worship God In Spirit And In Truth.

The Bible said, "20 Our fathers worshipped in this mountain; and ye say, that in Jerusalem is the place where men ought to worship. 21 Jesus saith unto her, Woman, believe me, the hour cometh, when ye shall neither in this mountain, nor yet at Jerusalem, worship the Father. 22 Ye worship ye know not what: we know what we worship: for salvation is of the Jews. 23 But the hour cometh, and now is, when the true worshippers shall worship the Father in spirit and in truth: for the Father seeketh such to worship him. 24 God is a Spirit: and they that worship him must worship him in spirit and in truth" John 4:20-24.

The Bible said, "10 For the Son of man is come to seek and to save that which was lost" Luke 19:10.

There Are Some People, Who Are Seeking: Rest For Their Souls.

The Bible said, "16 Thus saith the LORD, Stand ye in the ways, and see, and ask for the old paths, where is the good way, and walk therein, and ye shall find rest for your souls. But they said, We will not walk therein" Jer 6:16.

Jesus said, "28 Come unto me, all ye that labour and are heavy laden, and I will give you rest. 29 Take my yoke upon you, and learn of me; for I am meek and lowly in heart: and ye shall find rest unto your souls. 30 For my yoke is easy, and my burden is light" Matt 11:28-30.

There Are Some People, Who Are Seeking: Salvation For Their Souls.

The Bible said, "2 And, behold, there was a man named Zacchaeus, which was the chief among the publicans, and he was rich. 4 And he ran before, and climbed up into a sycamore tree to see him: for he was to pass that way. 5 And when Jesus came to the place, he looked up, and saw him, and said unto him, Zacchaeus, make haste, and come down; for to day I must abide at thy house. 9 And Jesus said unto him, This day is salvation come to this house, forsomuch as he also is a son of Abraham. 10 For the Son of man is come to seek and to save that which was lost" Luke 19:2, 4-5, 9-10.

Paul said, "10 Therefore I endure all things for the elect's sakes, that they may also obtain the salvation which is in Christ Jesus with eternal glory" 2 Tim 2:10.

Paul said, "10 Be it known unto you all, and to all the people of Israel, that by the name of Jesus Christ of Nazareth, whom ye crucified, whom God raised from the dead, even by him doth this man stand here before you whole. 11 This is the stone which was set at nought of you builders, which is become the head of the corner. 12 Neither is there salvation in any other: for there is none other name under heaven given among men, whereby we must be saved" Acts 4:10-12.

There Are Some People, Who Are Seeking Jesus: But They Do Not Believe In Him.

Jesus said, "21 Then said Jesus again unto them, I go my way, and ye shall seek me, and shall die in your sins: whither I go, ye cannot come. 24 I said therefore unto you, that ye shall die in your sins: for if ye believe not that I am he, ye shall die in your sins" John 8:21, 24.

Jesus said, "44 Ye are of your father the devil, and the lusts of your father ye will do. He was a murderer from the beginning, and abode not in the truth, because there is no truth in him. When he speaketh a lie, he speaketh of his own: for he is a liar, and the father of it.

45 And because I tell you the truth, ye believe me not" John 8:44-45.

Jesus said, "39 Search the scriptures; for in them ye think ye have eternal life: and they are they which testify of me. 40 And ye will not come to me, that ye might have life. 44 How can ye believe, which receive honour one of another, and seek not the honour that cometh from God only? John 5:39-40, 44.

Some People Are Seeking Spiritual Peace: In Their Life.

Jesus said, "21 He that hath my commandments, and keepeth them, he it is that loveth me: and he that loveth me shall be loved of my Father, and

I will love him, and will manifest myself to him. 23 Jesus answered and said unto him, If a man love me, he will keep my words: and my Father will love him, and we will come unto him, and make our abode with him. 24 He that loveth me not keepeth not my sayings: and the word which ye hear is not mine, but the Father's which sent me" John 14:21, 23-24.

Peter said, "10 For he that will love life, and see good days, let him refrain his tongue from evil, and his lips that they speak no guile: 11 Let him eschew evil, and do good; let him seek peace, and ensue it" 1 Peter 3:10-11.

Children Of God: Live Your Dream

Dreams: A series of images, and ideas, that you can see in your mind that you hope of achieving in your life time.

Dreams give ambition to a person's life.

Jeremiah said, "28 The prophet that hath a dream, let him tell a dream; and he that hath my word, let him speak my word faithfully. what is the chaff to the wheat? saith the lord" Jeremiah 23:28.

Joseph Was A Dreamer.

The Bible said, "16 And he said, I seek my brethren: tell me, I pray thee, where they feed their flocks. 17 And the man said, They are departed hence; for I heard them say, Let us go to Dothan. And Joseph went after his brethren, and found them in Dothan. 18 And when they saw him afar off, even before he came near unto them, they conspired against him to slay him. 19 And they said one to another, Behold, this dreamer cometh" Gen 37:16-19.

My Lifelong Dream Has Been: To Be A Teacher.

The Minister of the McAlmont church of Christ: started a preacher's seminar where he taught a group of young men how to study, and how to prepare sermons, and how to teach the Bible, and I was one of his students. After completing the seminar, I started teaching home bible classes and not long after that, the minister made me a Bible class teacher, at that time I knew that my dream of being a teacher had come true, and it was a great accomplishment to me, to have my dream to come true in the house of God.

Sometime when you are pursuing your dream: The people that you love and trust will be the ones that scheme against you, mainly because, they do not understand your ambitious or determine nature.

In 1983, The Minister of the Mcalmont church of Christ carried me to a church meeting that was held at the Scott Avenue church of Christ in Forrest City, Arkansas, during that meeting, they selected me to be the minister for that congregation.

That was the beginning of my ministry, and it took me many years to find out why the Minister from the Mcalmont church of Christ never did come to support me at the Scott Avenue church of Christ in Forrest City, Arkansas.

Paul said, "16 At my first answer no man stood with me, but all men forsook me: I pray God that it may not be laid to their charge" Tim 4:16.

Sometime, when you are following your dream: You may lose your countryman; your kinsfolk; and your familiar friends.

Jesus said, "57 And they were offended in him: But Jesus said unto them, a prophet is not without honour, save in his own country, and in his own house" Matt 13:57.

When your countryman; your kinsfolk; and your familiar friends have abandoned you, you continue to trust in God and share your dream with others. Always remember what the Bible said in the epistle of Job.

Job said, "14 My kinsfolk have failed, and my familiar friends have forgotten me.

15 They that dwell in mine house, and my maids, count me for a stranger: I am an alien in their sight" Job 19:14-15.

Paul said, "13 There hath no temptation taken you but such as is common to man: but God is faithful, who will not suffer you to be tempted above that ye are able; but will with the temptation also make a way to escape, that ye may be able to bear it" 1 Cor 10:13.

Christians: If you get to a point in your life while you are perusing your dream, and you feel despair, just lift up your eyes to God.

David said, "1 I will lift up mine eyes unto the hills, from whence cometh my help. 2 My help cometh from the LORD, which made heaven and earth. 3 He will not suffer thy foot to be moved: he that keepeth thee will not slumber" Psalms 121:1-3.

David said, "10 Create in me a clean heart, O God; and renew a right spirit within me. 11 Cast me not away from thy presence; and take not thy holy spirit from me. 12 Restore unto me the joy of thy salvation; and uphold me with thy free spirit. 13 Then will I teach transgressors thy ways; and sinners shall be converted unto thee" Psalms 51:10-13.

Christians: Must realize that there is trouble on every side, yet we must stay focus on our dream.

Paul said, "8 We are troubled on every side, yet not distressed; we are perplexed, but not in despair; 9 Persecuted, but not forsaken; cast down, but not destroyed; 10 Always bearing about in the body the dying of the Lord Jesus, that the life also of Jesus might be made manifest in our body" 2 Cor 4:8-10.

Stray Gospel Preachers

Stray gospel preachers: Are gospel preachers who have moved or have deviate from the course that God established!

Paul warned Timothy concerning stray gospel preachers.

Paul said, "1 Now the Spirit speaketh expressly, that in the latter times some shall depart from the faith, giving heed to seducing spirits, and doctrines of devils" 1 Tim 4:1.

Paul said, "13 But evil men and seducers shall wax worse and worse, deceiving, and being deceived" 2 Tim 3:13.

There are many stray gospel preachers, that have gone from the course that God established, and have gone about to establish their own righteousness.

Paul said, "1 Brethren, my heart's desire and prayer to God for Israel is, that they might be saved. 2 For I bear them record that they have a zeal of God, but not according to knowledge. 3 For they being ignorant of God's righteousness, and going about to establish their own righteousness, have not submitted themselves unto the righteousness of God" Romans 10:1-3.

There are many stray gospel preachers, which are causing many people to deviate from the course that God established.

Paul said, "6 I marvel that ye are so soon removed from him that called you into the grace of Christ unto another gospel: 7 Which is not another; but there be some that trouble you, and would pervert the gospel of Christ. 8 But though we, or an angel from heaven, preach any other gospel unto you than that which we have preached unto you, let him be accursed. 9 As we said before, so say I now again, If any man preach any other gospel unto you than that ye have received, let him be accursed" Gal 1:6-9.

Paul encourages the churches in Corinth: To stay on the course that God established, and to follow his teaching.

Paul said, "1 Be ye followers of me, even as I also am of Christ. 2 Now I praise you, brethren, that ye remember me in all things, and keep the ordinances, as I delivered them to you. 3 But I would have you know, that the head of every man is Christ; and the head of the woman is the man; and the head of Christ is God" 1 Cor 11:1-3.

There are many stray gospel preachers that have deviate from the ordinances of God, as Paul taught the church in Corinth that they were doing: By allowing women to teach in the church.

Paul said, "12 But I suffer not a woman to teach, nor to usurp authority over the man, but to be in silence. 13 For Adam was first formed, then Eve. 14 And Adam was not deceived, but the woman being deceived was in the transgression" 1 Tim 2:12-14.

God reprimanded the churches of Christ in Thyatira: For deviating from the course that he commanded them to follow.

The Bible said, "18 And unto the angel of the church in Thyatira write; These things saith the Son of God, who hath his eyes like unto a flame of fire, and his feet are like fine brass; 19 I know thy works, and charity, and service, and faith, and thy patience, and thy works; and the last to be more than the first. 20 Notwithstanding I have a few things against thee, because thou sufferest that woman Jezebel, which calleth herself a prophetess, to teach and to seduce my servants to commit fornication, and to eat things sacrificed unto idols" Rev 2:18-20.

There are many stray gospel preachers: That have deviate from the course that God established, concerning worshipping God on Sunday afternoon.

The Bible proves that Sunday afternoon worship is scriptural.

The Bible said, "1 Now Peter and John went up together into the temple at the hour of prayer, being the ninth hour. (That is 3 PM in the afternoon). 2 And a certain man lame from his mother's womb was carried, whom they laid daily at the gate of the temple which is called Beautiful, to ask alms of them that entered into the temple; 3 Who seeing Peter and John about to go into the temple asked an alms" Acts 3:1-3.

The Bible proves that on one Sunday Paul and some others worship God all night long.

The Bible said, "7 And upon the first day of the week, when the disciples came together to break bread, Paul preached unto them, ready to depart on the morrow; and continued his speech until midnight. 8 And there were many lights in the upper chamber, where they were gathered together. 9 And there sat in a window a certain young man named Eutychus, being fallen into a deep sleep: and as Paul was long preaching, he sunk down with sleep, and fell down from the third loft, and was taken up dead. 10 And Paul went down, and fell on him, and embracing him said, Trouble not yourselves; for his life is in him. 11 When he therefore was come up again, and had broken bread, and eaten, and talked a long while, even till break of day, so he departed" Acts 20:7-11.

There are many stray gospel preachers: Who have put their hands to the plough and are looking back.

The Bible said, "62 And Jesus said unto him, No man, having put his hand to the plough, and looking back, is fit for the kingdom of God" Luke 9:62.

Gospel Preachers: Who Have Retired, Or Is Intending To Retire

Retire: Is to withdraw from one's occupation, business, or office: Stop working or stop preaching.

There are some ungodly gospels preachers in the churches of Christ, who have allowed the devil to entice them to retire from preaching the gospel of Christ.

Jude said, "3 Beloved, when I gave all diligence to write unto you of the common salvation, it was needful for me to write unto you, and exhort you that ye should earnestly contend for the faith which was once delivered unto the saints. 4 For there are certain men crept in unawares, who were before of old ordained to this condemnation, ungodly men, turning the grace of our God into lasciviousness, and denying the only Lord God, and our Lord Jesus Christ" Jude 1:3-4.

There are some gospels preachers who have retired from preaching the gospel of Christ at certain local congregations and have become freelance gospel preachers, which mean that they can preach the gospel of Christ at various congregations for money.

Paul said, "9 But they that will be rich fall into temptation and a snare, and into many foolish and hurtful lusts, which drown men in destruction and perdition. 10 For the love of money is the root of all evil: which while some coveted after, they have erred from the faith, and pierced themselves through with many sorrows. 11 But thou, O man of God, flee these things; and follow after righteousness, godliness, faith, love, patience, meekness" 1 Tim 6:9-11.

Paul said, "2 Preach the word; be instant in season, out of season; reprove, rebuke, exhort with all longsuffering and doctrine. 3 For the time will come when they will not endure sound doctrine; but after their own lusts shall they heap to themselves teachers, having itching ears; 4 And they shall turn away their ears from the truth, and shall be turned unto fables. 5 But watch thou in all things, endure afflictions, do the work of an evangelist, make full proof of thy ministry" 2 Tim 4:2-5.

The Prophet Jeremiah: Thought that he had a reason to stop preaching the word of God, and look at what God did to him. Then what does these modern-day preachers think that God will do to them?

The Bible said, "7 O LORD, thou hast deceived me, and I was deceived: thou art stronger than I, and hast prevailed: I am in derision daily, every one mocketh me. 8 For since I spake, I cried out, I cried violence and spoil; because the word of the LORD was made a reproach unto me, and a derision, daily. 9 Then I said, I will not make mention of him, nor speak any more in his name. But his word was in mine heart as a burning fire shut up in my bones, and I was weary with forbearing, and I could not stay" Jer 20:7-9.

God told the Prophet Isaiah how long to preach his word.

Isaiah said, "8 Also I heard the voice of the Lord, saying, Whom shall I send, and who will go for us? Then said I, Here am I; send me. 9 And he said, Go, and tell this people, Hear ye indeed, but understand not; and see ye indeed, but perceive not. 10 Make the heart of this people fat, and make their ears heavy, and shut their eyes; lest they see with their eyes, and hear with their ears, and understand with their heart, and convert, and be healed. 11 Then said I, Lord, how long? And he answered, Until the cities be wasted without inhabitant, and the houses without man, and the land be utterly desolate, 12 And the LORD have removed men far away, and there be a great forsaking in the midst of the land" Isaiah 6:8-12.

The Apostle Paul told Timothy: That he was going to preach the word of God until his death.

Paul said, "6 For I am now ready to be offered, and the time of my departure is at hand.

7 I have fought a good fight, I have finished my course, I have kept the faith: 8 Henceforth there is laid up for me a crown of righteousness, which the Lord, the righteous judge, shall give me at that day: and not to me only, but unto all them also that love his appearing" 2 Tim 4:6-8.

Men and Brethren: The Bible teaches that every gospel preacher is to speak as the oracles of God; and there is no place in the scriptures where the Bible teaches that gospel preachers can retire from preaching the word of God.

Peter said, "10 As every man hath received the gift, even so minister the same one to another, as good stewards of the manifold grace of God. 11 If any man speak, let him speak as the oracles of God; if any man minister, let him do it as of the ability which God giveth: that God in all things may be glorified through Jesus Christ, to whom be praise and dominion for ever and ever. Amen.

12 Beloved, think it not strange concerning the fiery trial which is to try you, as though some strange thing happened unto you: 13 But rejoice, inasmuch as ye are partakers of Christ's sufferings; that, when his glory shall be revealed, ye may be glad also with exceeding joy" 1 Peter 4:10-13.

The Bible teaches that Christ is our example: And he worked until he died.

Peter said, "21 For even hereunto were ye called: because Christ also suffered for us, leaving us an example, that ye should follow his steps: 22 Who did no sin, neither was guile found in his mouth" 1 Peter 2:21-22.

Jesus said, "4 I must work the works of him that sent me, while it is day: the night cometh, when no man can work. 5 As long as I am in the world, I am the light of the world" John 9:4-5.

The Bible said, "59 And he said unto another, Follow me. But he said, Lord, suffer me first to go and bury my father. 60 Jesus said unto him, Let the dead bury their dead: but go thou and preach the kingdom of God. 61 And another also said, Lord, I will follow thee; but let me first go bid them farewell, which are at home at my house. 62 And Jesus said unto him, No man, having put his hand to the plough, and looking back, is fit for the kingdom of God" Luke 9:59-62.

Some Things That Satan: Has Sifted Out Of The People Of God

Sifter: For example; is a straining device: To put flour through a sieve or other in order to separate the fine from the coarse particles.

The Devil: Uses his sifter or his straining device, to separate the Good from the Evil, out of the people of God.

The Bible said, "31 And the Lord said, Simon, Simon, behold, Satan hath desired to have you, that he may sift you as wheat: 32 But I have prayed for thee, that thy faith fail not: and when thou art converted, strengthen thy brethren" Luke 22:31-32.

Satan has sifted: Coming to God's house of prayer out of the hearts of many Christians.

The Bible said, "7 Even them will I bring to my holy mountain, and make them joyful in my house of prayer: their burnt offerings and their sacrifices shall be accepted upon mine altar; for mine house shall be called an house of prayer for all people. 8 The Lord GOD which gathereth the outcasts of Israel saith, Yet will I gather others to him, beside those that are gathered unto him" Isaiah 56:7-8.

The Bible said, "12 And Jesus went into the temple of God, and cast out all them that sold and bought in the temple, and overthrew the tables of the moneychangers, and the seats of them that sold doves, 13 And said unto them, It is written, My house shall be called the house of prayer; but ye have made it a den of thieves" Matt 21:12-13.

Jesus said, "13 But woe unto you, scribes and Pharisees, hypocrites! for ye shut up the kingdom of heaven against men: for ye neither go in yourselves, neither suffer ye them that are entering to go in" Matt 23:13.

Satan has sifted: The head of the wife out of many Christian's homes.

Paul said, "1 Be ye followers of me, even as I also am of Christ. 2 Now I praise you, brethren, that ye remember me in all things, and keep the ordinances, as I delivered them to you. 3 But I would have you know, that the head of every man is Christ; and the head of the woman is the man; and the head of Christ is God" 1 Cor 11:1-3.

Paul said, "22 Wives, submit yourselves unto your own husbands, as unto the Lord. 23 For the husband is the head of the wife, even as Christ is the head of the church: and he is the saviour of the body. 24 Therefore as the church is subject unto Christ, so let the wives be to their own husbands in every thing" Eph 5:22-24.

Satan has sifted: Forgetting the past out of the hearts of many Christians.

Paul said, "13 Brethren, I count not myself to have apprehended: but this one thing I do, forgetting those things which are behind, and reaching forth unto those things which are before, 14 I press toward the mark for the prize of the high calling of God in Christ Jesus. 15 Let us therefore, as many as be perfect, be thus minded: and if in any thing ye be otherwise minded, God shall reveal even this unto you. 16 Nevertheless, whereto we have already attained, let us walk by the same rule, let us mind the same thing" Phil 3:13-16.

Satan has sifted: Love one another out of the hearts of many Christians.

Peter said, "22 Seeing ye have purified your souls in obeying the truth through the Spirit unto unfeigned love of the brethren, see that ye love one another with a pure heart fervently:

23 Being born again, not of corruptible seed, but of incorruptible, by the word of God, which liveth and abideth for ever"1 Peter 1:22-23.

The Bible said, "14 We know that we have passed from death unto life, because we love the brethren. He that loveth not his brother abideth in death. 15 Whosoever hateth his brother is a murderer: and ye know that no murderer hath eternal life abiding in him. 16 Hereby perceive we the love of God, because he laid down his life for us: and we ought to lay down our lives for the brethren. 17 But whoso hath this world's good, and seeth his brother have need, and shutteth up his bowels of compassion from him, how dwelleth the love of God in him? 18 My little children, let us not love in word, neither in tongue; but in deed and in truth"1 John 3:14-18.

Satan has sifted: Believing the word of God out of the hearts of many people.

Jesus said, "37 If I do not the works of my Father, believe me not. 38 But if I do, though ye believe not me, believe the works: that ye may know, and believe, that the Father is in me, and I in him" John 10:37-38.

Jesus said, "1 Let not your heart be troubled: ye believe in God, believe also in me. 10 Believest thou not that I am in the Father, and the Father in me? the words that I speak unto you I speak not of myself: but the Father that dwelleth in me, he doeth the works. 11 Believe me that I am in the Father, and the Father in me: or else believe me for the very works' sake" John 14:1, 10-11.

Paul said, "3 For what if some did not believe? shall their unbelief make the faith of God without effect? 4 God forbid: yea, let God be true, but every man a liar; as it is written, That thou mightest be justified in thy sayings, and mightest overcome when thou art judged" Romans 3:3-4.

The Bible said, "36 What manner of saying is this that he said, Ye shall seek me, and shall not find me: and where I am, thither ye cannot come? 37 In the last day, that great day of the feast, Jesus stood and cried, saying, If any man thirst, let him come unto me, and drink. 38 He that believeth on me, as the scripture hath said, out of his belly shall flow rivers of living water" John 7:36-38.

The Bible said, "21 Then said Jesus again unto them, I go my way, and ye shall seek me, and shall die in your sins: whither I go, ye cannot come. 24 I said therefore unto you, that ye shall die in your sins: for if ye believe not that I am he, ye shall die in your sins" John 8:21, 24.

Black People History: In White America

In White America: Black People are similar to what Paul told the church in Corinth, when he said, "we are troubled on every side".

Paul said, "8 We are troubled on every side, yet not distressed; we are perplexed, but not in despair; 9 Persecuted, but not forsaken; cast down, but not destroyed" 2 Cor 4:8-9.

In White America: White men have given Black People, one month out of 12 to remember their history.

I want to impress upon the hearts of all Black People who are living in White America; that Black People should remember their history in White America every day of our lives, because being Black is a God given honor that no man can take from us.

From the days of Adam and Eve, until Babel; all the people in the world spoke the same language.

It was at Babel, where God separated the people to live in all parts of the world, and God did not separate the people by the color of their skin, he separated them by their languages.

The Bible said, "6 And the LORD said, Behold, the people is one, and they have all one language; and this they begin to do: and now nothing will be restrained from them, which they have imagined to do. 7 Go to, let us go down, and there confound their language, that they may not understand one another's speech. 8 So the LORD scattered them abroad from thence upon the face of all the earth: and they left off to build the city" Gen 11:6-8.

Black People must never forget: That Black People were stolen from our native homelands and brought to White America where we were sold as slaves.

Black People must never forget: That some Black People were sold as slaves to work as pack horses, building railroads, and many other strenuous backbreaking jobs.

Black People must never forget: The struggles, the distress, and the hardships that Black People have gone and are going through here in White America.

Black People must never forget: That some Black People was sold as slaves to work in the white slave-master homes.

Black People must never forget: That some Black Men were sold as slaves to protect the white slave-masters females from danger, while the slave-masters was gone away from home, but before they could do so, the slave-masters would have those Black Men castrated so that they were unable to engage in any sexual intercourses with their white females.

Black People must never forget: Those long agonizing years, living on those White Sharecropper's Plantations, when during the cotton chopping seasons, grown-ups and teenagers were paid $3.00 per a 12 hour day, (approx) $.25 per hour. And the little children from six years old until they became teenagers was being paid $1.50 per a 12 hour day, (approx) $.12 per hour.

On those White Sharecropper's Plantations during the cotton picking season, Black People were being paid $.50 per a hundred pounds of cotton. And the grown men who were operating farm tractors, cotton pickers, combines, and other types of farm machinery was paid $5.00 per a 12 hour day, (approx) $.41 per hour.

Black People must never forget: Those barriers that the White People put up showing their discrimination against Black People here in White America.

Black People must never forget: That we could not eat in the White Man restaurants. We could not go into a White Man house through the front door. We could not go to the White Man schools. We could not go to the White Man public bathrooms. We could not go to the White Man movie theater and sit in the same area with the White People. We could not drink water from the White Man water fountains, yes here in White America.

Black People must never forget: That we could buy gasoline from the White Man gasoline stations, but we could not pay for it in front of the gasoline stations, in most places Black People had to go to the back of the gasoline stations to pay for the gasoline.

Black People must never forget: Those awful things that were done to us by those malicious racial hate groups, who were killing and are still killing Black People here in White America.

Black People must never forget: Those awful years when Black Men, Women, and Children was being raped, shot, stabbed, and hung by the throat, by the Ku Klux Klan members, and other malicious racial hate groups, with no repercussion from the White Law enforcement agencies whatsoever, here in White America.

Black People must never forget: That some of the Ku Klux Klan members have exchanged their white sheets for some courtroom judge robes!

Black People must never forget: That some Ku Klux Klan members have exchanged their white sheets, and their illegal use of firearms, to receive some policeman's uniforms and badges issued to them by the White Law enforcement agencies, authorizing them to carry legal firearms that are still being used to kill Black People here in White America.

Black People must never forget: That we have never been called by our native name, while living in White America.

Black People have always been called by some awful races names given to us by the White People: Names such as, Uncle-Tom: Boy: Nigger: Negro: Blacks: Colored People: African Americans.

In these days, Black People are being called People of Color: Which is another races name, that Black People are been called while living in White America.

Black People and all other Ethnic Groups in the entire world must realize: For us to survive as a world, we must learn how to live in peace with one another, in the manner that Paul told the church in Rome.

Paul said, "17 Recompense to no man evil for evil. Provide things honest in the sight of all men. 18 If it be possible, as much as lieth in you, live peaceably with all men. 19 Dearly beloved, avenge not yourselves, but rather give place unto wrath: for it is written, Vengeance is mine; I will repay, saith the Lord. 20 Therefore if thine enemy hunger, feed him; if he thirst, give him drink: for in so doing thou shalt heap coals of fire on his head. 21 Be not overcome of evil, but overcome evil with good" Romans 12:17-21.

Paul said, "13 For, brethren, ye have been called unto liberty; only use not liberty for an occasion to the flesh, but by love serve one another. 14 For all the law is fulfilled in one word, even in this; Thou shalt love thy neighbour as thyself. 15 But if ye bite and devour one another, take heed that ye be not consumed one of another. 16 This I say then, Walk in the Spirit, and ye shall not fulfil the lust of the flesh. 17 For the flesh lusteth against the Spirit, and the Spirit against the flesh: and these are contrary the one to the other: so that ye cannot do the things that ye would" Gal 5:13-17.

Black People must never forget: That it was the grace of God, that helped us to survived the hardships and other horrendous things that we have been put through and are still being put through while living in White America.

Men and Brethrens; I am not insensitive nor naïve concerning the things that Black People have gone through and are still going through here in White America; yet the truth must be told because according to Jesus the truth shall make you free.

Jesus said, "32 And Ye Shall Know The Truth, And The Truth Shall Make You Free. 36 If The Son Therefore Shall Make You Free, Ye Shall Be Free Indeed" John 8:32, 36.

Walk Out On Faith

Walking out on faith: Is like a believer of the word of God, taking a quantum leap into spiritually.

The Bible said, "1 Now faith is the substance of things hoped for, the evidence of things not seen. 6 But without faith it is impossible to please him: for he that cometh to God must believe that he is, and that he is a rewarder of them that diligently seek him" Heb 11:1, 6.

Abraham: Walked out on faith, when God told him to offer his son for a burnt offering.

The Bible said, "1 And it came to pass after these things, that God did tempt Abraham, and said unto him, Abraham: and he said, Behold, here I am. 2 And he said, Take now thy son, thine only son Isaac, whom thou lovest, and get thee into the land of Moriah; and offer him there for a burnt offering upon one of the mountains which I will tell thee of. 3 And Abraham rose up early in the morning, and saddled his ass, and took two of his young men with him, and Isaac his son, and clave the wood for the burnt offering, and rose up, and went unto the place of which God had told him" Gen 22:1-3.

Isaac: Walked out on faith, when his father told him that God will provide himself a lamb for a burnt offering.

The Bible said, "7 And Isaac spake unto Abraham his father, and said, My father: and he said, Here am I, my son. And he said, Behold the fire and the wood: but where is the lamb for a burnt offering? 8 And Abraham said, My son, God will provide himself a lamb for a burnt offering: so they went both of them together. 9 And they came to the place which God had told him of; and Abraham built an altar there, and laid the wood in order, and bound Isaac his son, and laid him on the altar upon the wood. 10 And Abraham stretched forth his hand, and took the knife to slay his son" Gen 22:7-10.

Peter: Walked out on faith, when Christ told him to launch out into the deep.

The Bible said, "3 And he entered into one of the ships, which was Simon's, and prayed him that he would thrust out a little from the land. And he sat down, and taught the people out of the ship. 4 Now when he had left speaking, he said unto Simon, Launch out into the deep, and let down your nets for a draught. 5 And Simon answering said unto him, Master, we have toiled all the night, and have taken nothing: nevertheless at thy word I will let down the net. 6 And when they had this done, they inclosed a great multitude of fishes: and their net brake. 7 And they beckoned unto their partners, which were in the other ship, that they should come and help them. And they came, and filled both the ships, so that they began to sink" Luke 5:3-7.

Peter: Walked out on faith, when Christ told him to come to him on the water.

The Bible said, "25 And in the fourth watch of the night Jesus went unto them, walking on the sea. 26 And when the disciples saw him walking on the sea, they were troubled, saying, It is a spirit; and they cried out for fear. 27 But straightway Jesus spake unto them, saying, Be of good cheer; it is I; be not afraid. 28 And Peter answered him and said, Lord, if it be thou, bid me come unto thee on the water. 29 And he said, Come. And when Peter was come down out of the ship, he walked on the water, to go to Jesus" Matt 14:25-29.

The Woman with an issue of blood: Walked out on faith.

The Bible said, "20 And, behold, a woman, which was diseased with an issue of blood twelve years, came behind him, and touched the hem of his garment: 21 For she said within herself, If I may but touch his garment, I shall be whole" Matt 9:20-21.

Isaiah: Walked out on faith, when he heard the voice of the Lord.

The Bible said, "8 Also I heard the voice of the Lord, saying, Whom shall I send, and who will go for us? Then said I, Here am I; send me. 9 And he said, Go, and tell this people, Hear ye indeed, but understand not; and see ye indeed, but perceive not; Isaiah 6:8-9.

Paul: Walked out on faith, when Christ told him that he was going to make him a minister and a witness.

The Bible said, "13 At midday, O king, I saw in the way a light from heaven, above the brightness of the sun, shining round about me and them which journeyed with me. 14 And when we were all fallen to the earth, I heard a voice speaking unto me, and saying in the Hebrew tongue, Saul, Saul, why persecutest thou me? it is hard for thee to kick against the pricks. 15 And I said, Who art thou, Lord? And he said, I am Jesus whom thou persecutest. 16 But rise, and stand upon thy feet: for I have appeared unto thee for this purpose, to make thee a minister and a witness both of these things which thou hast seen, and of those things in the which I will appear unto thee; 19 Whereupon, O king Agrippa, I was not disobedient unto the heavenly vision" Acts 26:13-16, 19.

The Entire World: Needs to walk out on faith of the word of God.

Paul said, "17 So then faith cometh by hearing, and hearing by the word of God. 18 But I say, Have they not heard? Yes verily, their sound went into all the earth, and their words unto the ends of the world. 19 But I say, Did not Israel know? First Moses saith, I will provoke you to jealousy by them that are no people, and by a foolish nation I will anger you. 20 But Esaias is very bold, and saith, I was found of them that sought me not; I was made manifest unto them that asked not after me" Romans 10:17-20.

God said, "11 So shall my word be that goeth forth out of my mouth: it shall not return unto me void, but it shall accomplish that which I please, and it shall prosper in the thing whereto I sent it. 12 For ye shall go out with joy, and be led forth with peace: the mountains and the hills shall break forth before you into singing, and all the trees of the field shall clap their hands. 13 Instead of the thorn shall come up the fir tree, and instead of the brier shall come up the myrtle tree: and it shall be to the LORD for a name, for an everlasting sign that shall not be cut off" Isaiah 55:11-13.

Black Christians Leaving: The Black Congregations Of The Churches Of Christ

I hope that I can impress upon the hearts of all Black Christians in the churches of Christ of the distress and the hardship that some black congregations are going through, because of them leaving the black congregations to ruin.

Nehemiah said, "17 Then said I unto them, Ye see the distress that we are in, how Jerusalem lieth waste, and the gates thereof are burned with fire: come, and let us build up the wall of Jerusalem, that we be no more a reproach" Neh 2:17.

I am hoping that all Black Christians will stop leaving the Black Congregations to ruin; simply because they are having problems in their congregations; whether they are trivial or doctrinal, instead of leaving the congregations, there should have been at least one brother in those congregations who could have arbitrate between his brethren and help them to resolved those problems between themselves without having to leave the congregation.

There was a times when Black People, lived in the Black People Neighborhoods, and when God blessed them to become Doctors, Lawyers, Professional Athletes, or some other type of Entrepreneurs, at that time some Black People moved to the White Neighborhoods leaving the Black Congregations and the people to ruin.

In some cases, the White People would develop new subdivisions out in the suburbs trying to get away from Black People, and yet many Black People moved into the White People Subdivisions that the White People develop for themselves.

My question is: Instead of the Black People following after the White People and moving into the White People Subdivisions leaving the Black people to ruin; Why did they not stay and work together using their Educational status and financial contributions to build and improve their own Neighborhoods, their Schools, their Congregations, other Recreational activities for their Children, and for other Underprivileged people that live in their Neighborhoods.

There are some Black Entrepreneurs who are still living in Black neighborhoods, but they have moved their membership from the Black Congregations and placed it with the White Congregations, Unfortunately those people has also cause the Black Congregations and their Neighborhoods to go to ruin.

I can remember when some Black families would send their children off to College to further their Education; so that they can bring the things home that they have learn in College; to help their people and other people who was living in their communities; to improve their way of life.

There are some of our young Black People who have gone to College and when they received their College Degree they did not come home to help their Black People in their communities; instead they went to the White People Neighborhoods, and lived among them, this too no doubt is another way of leaving the Black People and their Neighborhoods in ruin.

John said, "17 But whoso hath this world's good, and seeth his Brother Have Need, and shutteth up his bowels of Compassion from him, how dwelleth the Love Of God In Him? 18 My little children, let us not love in word, neither in tongue; but in Deed and in Truth" 1 John 3:17-18.

Like Nehemiah: I believe that we, the Black Christians can rise up and work together and rebuild our Congregations of the churches of Christ that has been left in ruin.

Nehemiah said, "17 Then said I unto them, Ye see the distress that we are in, how Jerusalem lieth waste, and the gates thereof are burned with fire: come, and let us build up the wall of Jerusalem, that we be no more a reproach. 18 Then I told them of the hand of my God which was good upon me; as also the king's words that he had spoken unto me. And they said, Let us rise up and build. So they strengthened their hands for this good work" Neh 2:17-18.

Paul told the church of Christ in Corinth: That God will make a way for them to escape.

Paul said, "13 There hath no temptation taken you but such as is common to man: but God is faithful, who will not suffer you to be tempted above that ye are able; but will with the temptation also make a way to escape, that ye may be able to bear it" 1 Cor 10:13.

Jesus taught his disciples; that if they give as God require: Then men will give unto them the same way.

Jesus said, "38 Give, and it shall be given unto you; good measure, pressed down, and shaken together, and running over, shall men give into your bosom. For with the same measure that ye mete withal it shall be measured to you again" Luke 6:38.

Based on what Paul told the church of Christ in Corinth, concerning God making a way: and based on what Jesus taught concerning men giving unto you.

There were several church buildings that were previously owned by White People and they sold those buildings to Black People who could not afford to buy land and have new buildings built on it.

The Bible said, "5 Let your conversation be without covetousness; and be content with such things as ye have: for he hath said, I will never leave thee, nor forsake thee. 6 So that we may boldly say, The Lord is my helper, and I will not fear what man shall do unto me" Heb 13:5-6.

Men and brethren: My Prayers to God is that Black People will come together so that we can build church buildings; build better communities, better neighborhoods, and a better world for all mankind.

Aliens: In A Strange Land

Aliens: Are foreigners or strangers in a strange place.

Abraham: Was an Alien in a strange land.

The Bible said, "8 By faith Abraham, when he was called to go out into a place which he should after receive for an inheritance, obeyed; and he went out, not knowing whither he went. 9 By faith he sojourned in the land of promise, as in a strange country, dwelling in tabernacles with Isaac and Jacob, the heirs with him of the same promise: 10 For he looked for a city which hath foundations, whose builder and maker is God. 13 These all died in faith, not having received the promises, but having seen them afar off, and were persuaded of them, and embraced them, and confessed that they were strangers and pilgrims on the earth" Heb 11:8-10, 13.

Job: Was an Alien in his own house.

The Bible said, "15 They that dwell in mine house, and my maids, count me for a stranger: I am an alien in their sight. 16 I called my servant, and he gave me no answer; I intreated him with my mouth. 17 My breath is strange to my wife, though I intreated for the children's sake of mine own body. 18 Yea, young children despised me; I arose, and they spake against me. 19 All my inward friends abhorred me: and they whom I loved are turned against me" Job 19:15-19.

Christ: Was an Alien in a strange land.

The Bible said, "56 For the Son of man is not come to destroy men's lives, but to save them. And they went to another village. 57 And it came to pass, that, as they went in the way, a certain man said unto him, Lord, I will follow thee whithersoever thou goest. 58 And Jesus said unto him, Foxes have holes, and birds of the air have nests; but the Son of man hath not where to lay his head" Luke 9:56-58.

There are some people who are alienated: From the life of God.

Paul said, "17 This I say therefore, and testify in the Lord, that ye henceforth walk not as other Gentiles walk, in the vanity of their mind, 18 Having the understanding darkened, being alienated from the life of God through the ignorance that is in them, because of the blindness of their heart: 19 Who being past feeling have given themselves over unto lasciviousness, to work all uncleanness with greediness" Eph 4:17-19.

Sinners Are strangers And foreigners: In the world.

Paul said, "19 For it pleased the Father that in him should all fulness dwell; 20 And, having made peace through the blood of his cross, by him to reconcile all things unto himself; by him, I say, whether they be things in earth, or things in heaven. 21 And you, that were sometime alienated and enemies in your mind by wicked works, yet now hath he reconciled. 22 In the body of his flesh through death, to present you holy and unblameable and unreproveable in his sight: 23 If ye continue in the faith grounded and settled, and be not moved away from the hope of the gospel, which ye have heard, and which was preached to every creature which is under heaven; whereof I Paul am made a minister" Col 1:19-23.

The Bible said, "17 And came and preached peace to you which were afar off, and to them that were nigh. 18 For through him we both have access by one Spirit unto the Father. 19 Now therefore ye are no more strangers and foreigners, but fellowcitizens with the saints, and of the household of God; 20 And are built upon the foundation of the apostles and prophets, Jesus Christ himself being the chief corner stone; 21 In whom all the building fitly framed together groweth unto an holy temple in the Lord:

22 In whom ye also are builded together for an habitation of God through the Spirit" Eph 2:17-22.

Paul said, "6 For when we were yet without strength, in due time Christ died for the ungodly. 7 For scarcely for a righteous man will one die: yet peradventure for a good man some would even dare to die. 8 But God commendeth his love toward us, in that, while we were yet sinners, Christ died for us. 9 Much more then, being now justified by his blood, we shall be saved from wrath through him. 10 For if, when we were enemies, we were reconciled to God by the death of his Son, much more, being reconciled, we shall be saved by his life. 11 And not only so, but we also joy in God through our Lord Jesus Christ, by whom we have now received the atonement" Romans 5:6-11.

Paul said, "16 know ye not, that to whom ye yield yourselves servants to obey, his servants ye are to whom ye obey; whether of sin unto death, or of obedience unto righteousness? 17 But God be thanked, that ye were the servants of sin, but ye have obeyed from the heart that form of doctrine which was delivered you. 18 Being then made free from sin, ye became the servants of righteousness" Romans 6:16-18.

When Moses was reunited with his family after he came back from Egypt; one of his sons said I have been an alien in a strange land.

The Bible said, "1 When Jethro, the priest of Midian, Moses' father in law, heard of all that God had done for Moses, and for Israel his people, and that the LORD had brought Israel out of Egypt; 2 Then Jethro, Moses' father in law, took Zipporah, Moses' wife, after he had sent her back, 3 And her two sons; of which the name of the one was Gershom; for he said, I have been an alien in a strange land" Ex 18:1-3.

Aliens: are also people who are not included in a group; this is the category that I am in, when it comes to Most Gospel Preachers, to Most of My Brothers and Sisters, to Most of My Relatives, and to Most of The Christians that I know.

Being an Alien does not necessarily mean that you have sinned: Because sometime people will alienate you because they have exiled themselves from you, which could be a sin on their part. Therefore my prayer to God is that if this is a sin on these other people part, that he will not lay this sin to their charge.

Learn Better: Do Better

Learn Better: Do better is a Spiritual, Cultural, and Educational Phrase: It is a Motivational Phrase; that can motivate people to do the best that they can do: And be the best that they can be.

Christ gave a Motivational speech: To all of the workers in the kingdom of God.

Christ said, "28 Come unto me, all ye that labour and are heavy laden, and I will give you rest. 29 Take my yoke upon you, and learn of me; for I am meek and lowly in heart: and ye shall find rest unto your souls. 30 For my yoke is easy, and my burden is light" Matt 11:28-30.

Christ gave a Motivational speech: To the entire world.

Christ said, "44 No man can come to me, except the Father which hath sent me draw him: and I will raise him up at the last day. 45 It is written in the prophets, And they shall be all taught of God. Every man therefore that hath heard, and hath learned of the Father, cometh unto me" John 6:44-45.

Solomon gave his son a Motivational speech.

Solomon said, "8 My son, hear the instruction of thy father, and forsake not the law of thy mother: 9 For they shall be an ornament of grace unto thy head, and chains about thy neck. 10 My son, if sinners entice thee, consent thou not" Prov 1:8-10.

Solomon said, "1 My son, forget not my law; but let thine heart keep my commandments: 2 For length of days, and long life, and peace, shall they add to thee. 3 Let not mercy and truth forsake thee: bind them about thy neck; write them upon the table of thine heart: 4 So shalt thou find favour and good understanding in the sight of God and man. 5 Trust in the LORD with all thine heart; and lean not unto thine own understanding. 6 In all thy ways acknowledge him, and he shall direct thy paths" Prov 3:1-6.

Solomon said, "7 Be not wise in thine own eyes: fear the LORD, and depart from evil. 8 It shall be health to thy navel, and marrow to thy bones. 9 Honour the LORD with thy substance, and with the firstfruits of all thine increase: 10 So shall thy barns be filled with plenty, and thy presses shall burst out with new wine. 11 My son, despise not the chastening of the LORD; neither be weary of his correction: 12 For whom the LORD loveth he correcteth; even as a father the son in whom he delighteth" Prov 3:7-12.

Peter gave a Motivational speech: To some Christians.

Peter said, "1 Wherefore laying aside all malice, and all guile, and hypocrisies, and envies, and all evil speakings, 2 As newborn babes, desire the sincere milk of the word, that ye may grow thereby: 3 If so be ye have tasted that the Lord is gracious" 1 Peter 2:1-3.

Peter said, "5 And beside this, giving all diligence, add to your faith virtue; and to virtue knowledge; 6 And to knowledge temperance; and to temperance patience; and to patience godliness; 7 And to godliness brotherly kindness; and to brotherly kindness charity. 8 For if these things be in you, and abound, they make you that ye shall neither be barren nor unfruitful in the knowledge of our Lord Jesus Christ. 9 But he that lacketh these things is blind, and cannot see afar off, and hath forgotten that he was purged from his old sins. 10 Wherefore the rather, brethren, give diligence to make your calling and election sure: for if ye do these things, ye shall never fall: 11 For so an entrance shall be ministered unto you abundantly into the everlasting kingdom of our Lord and Saviour Jesus Christ" 2 Peter 1:5-11.

Paul gave a Motivational speech: To the church of Christ in Corinth, encouraging them to separate themselves for the unbelievers.

Paul said, "11 O ye Corinthians, our mouth is open unto you, our heart is enlarged. 12 Ye are not straitened in us, but ye are straitened in your own bowels. 13 Now for a recompence in the same, (I speak as unto my children,) be ye also enlarged. 14 Be ye not unequally yoked together with unbelievers: for what fellowship hath righteousness with unrighteousness? and what communion hath light with darkness? 15 And what concord hath Christ with Belial? or what part hath he that believeth with an infidel? 16 And what agreement hath the temple of God with idols? for ye are the temple of the living God; as God hath said, I will dwell in them, and walk in them; and I will be their God, and they shall be my people. 17 Wherefore come out from among them, and be ye separate, saith the Lord, and touch not the unclean thing; and I will receive you, 18 And will be a Father unto you, and ye shall be my sons and daughters, saith the Lord Almighty" 2 Cor 6:11-18.

Paul gave a Motivational speech: To the church of Christ in Ephesus, encouraging them to keep the unity of the Spirit in the bond of peace.

Paul said, "3 Endeavouring to keep the unity of the Spirit in the bond of peace. 4 There is one body, and one Spirit, even as ye are called in one hope of your calling; 5 One Lord, one faith, one baptism, 6 One God and Father of all, who is above all, and through all, and in you all" Eph 4:3-6.

Parents: We need to motivate our children to love God; while they are young.

The Bible said, "5 And thou shalt love the LORD thy God with all thine heart, and with all thy soul, and with all thy might. 6 And these words, which I command thee this day, shall be in thine heart: 7 And thou shalt teach them diligently unto thy children, and shalt talk of them when thou sittest in thine house, and when thou walkest by the way, and when thou liest down, and when thou risest up. 8 And thou shalt bind them for a sign upon thine hand, and they shall be as frontlets between thine eyes. 9

And thou shalt write them upon the posts of thy house, and on thy gates" Deut 6:5-9.

Parents: We need to motivate our children to obey God; while they are young.

The Bible said, "1 Remember now thy Creator in the days of thy youth, while the evil days come not, nor the years draw nigh, when thou shalt say, I have no pleasure in them" Eccl 12:1.

Parents: We need to motivate our children while they are unmarried, to care for the things that belong to the Lord.

Paul said, "32 But I would have you without carefulness. He that is unmarried careth for the things that belong to the Lord, how he may please the Lord: 33 But he that is married careth for the things that are of the world, how he may please his wife. 34 There is difference also between a wife and a virgin. The unmarried woman careth for the things of the Lord, that she may be holy both in body and in spirit: but she that is married careth for the things of the world, how she may please her husband" 1 Cor 7:32-34.

Parents: We need to teach and to motivate our children to love their husbands and their wives, before they get married.

Paul said, "22 Wives, submit yourselves unto your own husbands, as unto the Lord. 23 For the husband is the head of the wife, even as Christ is the head of the church: and he is the saviour of the body. 24 Therefore as the church is subject unto Christ, so let the wives be to their own husbands in every thing. 25 Husbands, love your wives, even as Christ also loved the church, and gave himself for it" Eph 5:22-25.

Parents: We need to motivate our children to obey their parents, while they are young.

Paul said, "1 Children, obey your parents in the Lord: for this is right. 2 Honour thy father and mother; (which is the first commandment with promise;) 3 That it may be well with thee, and thou mayest live long on the earth" Eph 6:1-3.

Solomon said, "6 Train up a child in the way he should go: and when he is old, he will not depart from it" Prov 22:6.

David said, "3 children are an heritage of the LORD: and the fruit of the womb is his reward. 4 As arrows are in the hand of a mighty man; so are children of the youth. 5 Happy is the man that hath his quiver full of them: they shall not be ashamed, but they shall speak with the enemies in the gate" Psalms 127:3-5.

Peter gave a Motivational speech: For all Christians.

Peter said, "15 But let none of you suffer as a murderer, or as a thief, or as an evildoer, or as a busybody in other men's matters. 16 Yet if any man suffer as a Christian, let him not be ashamed; but let him glorify God on this behalf" 1 Peter 4:15-16.

If You Could Hear Of Christ Again

If you could hear the word of Christ again: Would it cause you to make a change in your life or would you remain the same?

A man that was born blind: Heard the word of Christ and it changed his life completely.

The Bible said, "1 And as Jesus passed by, he saw a man which was blind from his birth. 11 He answered and said, A man that is called Jesus made clay, and anointed mine eyes, and said unto me, Go to the pool of Siloam, and wash: and I went and washed, and I received sight. 25 He answered and said, Whether he be a sinner or no, I know not: one thing I know, that, whereas I was blind, now I see" John 9:1, 11, 25.

If you could hear the word of Christ again: Would you be his disciple?

The Bible said, "31 Then said Jesus to those Jews which believed on him, If ye continue in my word, then are ye my disciples indeed; 32 And ye shall know the truth, and the truth shall make you free" John 8:31-32.

If you could hear the word of Christ again: Concerning the suffering that he went through for the entire world: Would you be his disciple?

The Bible said, "3 He is despised and rejected of men; a man of sorrows, and acquainted with grief: and we hid as it were our faces from him; he was despised, and we esteemed him not. 4 Surely he hath borne our griefs, and carried our sorrows: yet we did esteem him stricken, smitten of God, and afflicted. 5 But he was wounded for our transgressions, he was bruised for our iniquities: the chastisement of our peace was upon him; and with his stripes we are healed. 6 All we like sheep have gone astray; we have turned every one to his own way; and the LORD hath laid on him the iniquity of us all. 7 He was oppressed, and he was afflicted, yet he opened not his mouth: he is brought as a lamb to the slaughter, and as a sheep before her shearers is dumb, so he openeth not his mouth. 8 He was taken from prison and from judgment: and who shall declare his generation? for he was cut off out of the land of the living: for the transgression of my people was he stricken. 9 And he made his grave with the wicked, and with the rich in his death; because he had done no violence, neither was any deceit in his mouth" Isaiah 53:3-9.

If you could hear the word of Christ again: How he died, and that he was buried; and that he rose again according to the scriptures: Would you be his disciple?

Paul said, "1 Moreover, brethren, I declare unto you the gospel which I preached unto you, which also ye have received, and wherein ye stand; 2 By which also ye are saved, if ye keep in memory what I preached unto you, unless ye have believed in vain. 3 For I delivered unto you first of all that which I also received, how that Christ died for our sins according to the scriptures; 4 And that he was buried, and that he rose again the third day according to the scriptures" 1 Cor 15:1-4.

Paul said, "16 For I am not ashamed of the gospel of Christ: for it is the power of God unto salvation to every one that believeth; to the Jew first, and also to the Greek. 17 For therein is the righteousness of God revealed from faith to faith: as it is written, The just shall live by faith" Romans 1:16-17.

If you could hear the word of Christ again: That he is the good shepherd: Would you become a member of his fold?

Jesus said, "14 I am the good shepherd, and know my sheep, and am known of mine. 15 As the Father knoweth me, even so know I the Father: and I lay down my life for the sheep. 16 And other sheep I have, which are not of this fold: them also I must bring, and they shall hear my voice; and there shall be one fold, and one shepherd" John 10:14-16.

Peter said, "24 Who his own self bare our sins in his own body on the tree, that we, being dead to sins, should live unto righteousness: by whose stripes ye were healed. 25 For ye were as sheep going astray; but are now returned unto the Shepherd and Bishop of your souls" 1 Peter 2:24-25.

If you could hear the word of Christ again: Concerning the foundation or the church of Christ: Would you become a member of his church: Or would you remain the same?

Paul said, "10 According to the grace of God which is given unto me, as a wise masterbuilder, I have laid the foundation, and another buildeth thereon. But let every man take heed how he buildeth thereupon. 11 For other foundation can no man lay than that is laid, which is Jesus Christ. 12 Now if any man build upon this foundation gold, silver, precious stones, wood, hay, stubble; 13 Every man's work shall be made manifest: for the day shall declare it, because it shall be revealed by fire; and the fire shall try every man's work of what sort it is" 1 Cor 3:10-13.

The Bible said, "16 And Simon Peter answered and said, Thou art the Christ, the Son of the living God. 17 And Jesus answered and said unto him, Blessed art thou, Simon Barjona: for flesh and blood hath not revealed it unto thee, but my Father which is in heaven. 18 And I say also unto thee, That thou art Peter, and upon this rock I will build my church; and the gates of hell shall not prevail against it" Matt 16:16-18.

If you could hear the word of Christ again: Concerning pure religion: Would you become a member of his church: Or would you remain a member of one of the denominational religions?

James said, "27 Pure religion and undefiled before God and the Father is this, To visit the fatherless and widows in their affliction, and to keep himself unspotted from the world" James 1:27.

The Bible said, "7 Again, he limiteth a certain day, saying in David, To day, after so long a time; as it is said, To day if ye will hear his voice, harden not your hearts. 9 There remaineth therefore a rest to the people of God. 10 For he that is entered into his rest, he also hath ceased from his own works, as God did from his. 11 Let us labour therefore to enter into that rest, lest any man fall after the same example of unbelief" Heb 4:7, 9-11.

Three Degree's Of The Devil

The Devil uses three Primary Lustful strategies to deceive the people of God.

1: The Devil uses his lustful strategy: To steal the people minds away from the word of God: So that he can keep them in darkness.

2: The Devil uses his lustful strategy: To kill the spiritual influence of the people of God: So that their light will not shine to show others the way to God.

3: The Devil uses his lustful strategy: To cause the people of the world to destroy their souls; by not obeying the word of God.

Jesus said, "10 The thief cometh not, but for to steal, and to kill, and to destroy: I am come that they might have life, and that they might have it more abundantly" John 10:10.

The Devil: Caused Judas To Commit Spiritual And Physical Suicide: By Causing Him To Sell Out Jesus.

The Bible said, "3 Then Judas, which had betrayed him, when he saw that he was condemned, repented himself, and brought again the thirty pieces of silver to the chief priests and elders, 4 Saying, I have sinned in that I have betrayed the innocent blood. And they said, What is that to us? see thou to that. 5 And he cast down the pieces of silver in the temple, and departed, and went and hanged himself" Matt 27:3-5.

The Devil: Has caused many people of god to commit spiritual suicide: by allowing him to cause them to take the communion of Christ unworthily.

The Bible said, "50 This is the bread which cometh down from heaven, that a man may eat thereof, and not die. 51 I am the living bread which came down from heaven: if any man eat of this bread, he shall live for ever: and the bread that I will give is my flesh, which I will give for the life of the world. 52 The Jews therefore strove among themselves, saying, How can this man give us his flesh to eat? 53 Then Jesus said unto them, Verily, verily, I say unto you, Except ye eat the flesh of the Son of man, and drink his blood, ye have no life in you" John 6:50-53.

Paul said, "16 The cup of blessing which we bless, is it not the communion of the blood of Christ? The bread which we break, is it not the communion of the body of Christ? 17 For we being many are one bread, and one body: for we are all partakers of that one bread" 1 Cor 10:16-17.

Paul said, "27 Wherefore whosoever shall eat this bread, and drink this cup of the Lord, unworthily, shall be guilty of the body and blood of the Lord. 28 But let a man examine himself, and so let him eat of that bread, and drink of that cup. 29 For he that eateth and drinketh unworthily, eateth and drinketh damnation to himself, not discerning the Lord's body. 30 For this cause many are weak and sickly among you, and many sleep" 1 Cor 11:27-30.

The Devil: Has caused many people of God to commit spiritual suicide: by allowing him to steal the taste of the word of God out of their minds.

Peter said, "2 As newborn babes, desire the sincere milk of the word, that ye may grow thereby:

3 If so be ye have tasted that the Lord is gracious" 1 Peter 2:2-3.

The Bible said, "4 For it is impossible for those who were once enlightened, and have tasted of the heavenly gift, and were made partakers of the Holy Ghost, 5 And have tasted the good word of God, and the powers of the world to come, 6 If they shall fall away, to renew them again unto repentance; seeing they crucify to themselves the Son of God afresh, and put him to an open shame" Heb 6:4-6.

The Devil: Has caused many people of God to commit spiritual suicide: by allowing him to steal their hearts away from believing in God.

Jesus said, "8 This people draweth nigh unto me with their mouth, and honoureth me with their lips; but their heart is far from me. 9 But in vain they do worship me, teaching for doctrines the commandments of men" Matt 15:8-9.

The Bible said, "10 Jesus answered and said unto her, If thou knewest the gift of God, and who it is that saith to thee, Give me to drink; thou wouldest have asked of him, and he would have given thee living water. 11 The woman saith unto him, Sir, thou hast nothing to draw with, and the well is deep: from whence then hast thou that living water? 12 Art thou greater than our father Jacob, which gave us the well, and drank thereof himself, and his children, and his cattle? 13 Jesus answered and said unto her, Whosoever drinketh of this water shall thirst again: 14 But whosoever drinketh of the water that I shall give him shall never thirst; but the water that I shall give him shall be in him a well of water springing up into everlasting life" John 4:10-14.

The Devil: Has caused many people of God to commit spiritual suicide: by causing them to reject Jesus Christ the son of God and by rejecting the knowledge of God.

Jesus said, "48 He that rejecteth me, and receiveth not my words, hath one that judgeth him: the word that I have spoken, the same shall judge him in the last day. 49 For I have not spoken of myself; but the Father which sent me, he gave me a commandment, what I should say, and what I should speak. 50 And I know that his commandment is life everlasting: whatsoever I speak therefore, even as the Father said unto me, so I speak" John 12:48-50.

God said, "6 My people are destroyed for lack of knowledge: because thou hast rejected knowledge, I will also reject thee, that thou shalt be no priest to me: seeing thou hast forgotten the law of thy God, I will also forget thy children" Hosea 4:6.

Paul said, "1 Brethren, my heart's desire and prayers to God for Israel is, that they might be saved. 2 For I bear them record that they have a zeal of God, but not according to knowledge" Romans 10:1-2.

Brothers And Sisters

I am written this lesson hoping and praying that it will help to bring all Brothers And Sisters closer together, and that it will help them to gain a better relationship with one another, and with God.

Spiritually speaking, God's purpose for authorized families; is that **All Children** are to be **Born Into Families** that has a **Man;** and a **Woman;** that is **Married** to **One Another**, in the same home.

My Father and Mother had 18 children born into their marital union; and they taught us that we were all legitimate.

The Bible teaches us: To love our Biological Family.

John said, "20 If a man say, I love God, and hateth his brother, he is a liar: for he that loveth not his brother whom he hath seen, how can he love God whom he hath not seen? 21 And this commandment have we from him, That he who loveth God love his brother also" 1 John 4:20-21.

The Bible teaches us: That Christians are born into a spiritual Family.

Paul said "14 For this cause I bow my knees unto the Father of our Lord Jesus Christ,

15 Of whom the whole family in heaven and earth is named" Eph 3:14-15,

Peter said, "5 Ye also, as lively stones, are built up a spiritual house, an holy priesthood, to offer up spiritual sacrifices, acceptable to God by Jesus Christ" 1 Peter 2:5.

Paul said, "9 But as touching brotherly love ye need not that I write unto you: for ye yourselves are taught of God to love one another" 1 Thess 4:9.

Even thou our parents and the Bible taught us to love one another: We have Brothers and Sisters in our Biological family, who are also members of the church of Christ family, and some of us do not have any Biological nor Spiritual connection with one another; regardless to what our parents or what God have said.

The Bible teaches us: Brothers And Sisters Are Born to Love One Another in Hardships, in Difficulties, and in Misfortune.

John said, "17 But Whoso Hath This World's Good, And Seeth His Brother Have Need, And Shutteth Up His Bowels Of Compassion From Him, How Dwelleth The Love Of God In Him? 18 My Little Children, Let Us Not Love In Word, Neither In Tongue; But In Deed And In Truth" 1 John 3:17-18.

There are many misfortunes that can cause family members to separate from one another: Such as with Esau and his Brother, Jacob.

The Bible said, "41 And Esau hated Jacob because of the blessing wherewith his father blessed him: and Esau said in his heart, The days of mourning for my father are at hand; then will I slay my brother Jacob. 42 And these words of Esau her elder son were told to Rebekah: and she sent and called Jacob her younger son, and said unto him, Behold, thy brother Esau, as touching thee, doth comfort himself, purposing to kill thee. 43 Now therefore, my son, obey my voice; and arise, flee thou to Laban my brother to Haran; 44 And tarry with him a few days, until thy brother's fury turn away" Gen 27:41-44.

Brothers and Sisters: Who have unsettled differences among themselves; should come together and be reconciled to one another; as Jacob and his brother Esau Did.

The Bible said, "1 And Jacob Lifted Up His Eyes, And Looked, And, Behold, Esau Came, And With Him Four Hundred Men. And He Divided The Children Unto Leah, And Unto Rachel, And Unto The Two Handmaids. 2 And He Put The Handmaids And Their Children Foremost, And Leah And Her Children After, And Rachel And Joseph Hindermost. 3 And He Passed Over Before Them, And Bowed Himself To The Ground Seven Times, Until He Came Near To His Brother. 4 And Esau Ran To Meet Him, And Embraced Him, And Fell On His Neck, And Kissed Him: And They Wept" Gen 33:1-4.

Jesus said, "23 Therefore if thou bring thy gift to the altar, and there rememberest that thy brother hath ought against thee; 24 Leave there thy gift before the altar, and go thy way; first be reconciled to thy brother, and then come and offer thy gift. 25 Agree with thine adversary quickly, whiles thou art in the way with him; lest at any time the adversary deliver thee to the judge, and the judge deliver thee to the officer, and thou be cast into prison" Matt 5:23-25.

Brothers and Sisters: We need to work together, to help save one another soul, from spending eternity in hell, before we die.

The Bible said, "23 And in hell he lift up his eyes, being in torments, and seeth Abraham afar off, and Lazarus in his bosom. 27 Then he said, I pray thee therefore, father, that thou wouldest send him to my father's house: 28 For I have five brethren; that he may testify unto them, lest they also come into this place of torment. 29 Abraham saith unto him, They have Moses and the prophets; let them hear them. 30 And he said, Nay, father Abraham: but if one went unto them from the dead, they will repent. 31 And he said unto him, If they hear not Moses and the prophets, neither will they be persuaded, though one rose from the dead" Luke 16:23, 27-31.

My Prayer To God Is: That all brothers and sisters will come to the realization; that the more there are in a family; the more they can achieve.

Solomon said, "9 Two are better than one; because they have a good reward for their labour. 10 For if they fall, the one will lift up his fellow: but woe to him that is alone when he falleth; for he hath not another to help him up. 11 Again, if two lie together, then they have heat: but how can one be warm alone? 12 And if one prevail against him, two shall withstand him; and a threefold cord is not quickly broken" Eccl 4:9-12.

The Black Hebrew Israelites

I wrote this epistle hoping to inform the entire world concerning the horrendous things that has happen to many people in the world; because of Cult leaders and their gang members!

The Critics In Israel Labeled The Black Hebrew Israelites A "Cult".

Gospel preachers: Are to teach God's people the difference between the holy and profane.

God said, "23 And they shall teach my people the difference between the holy and profane, and cause them to discern between the unclean and the clean" Ezek 44:23.

Gospel preachers: Are to defend the Gospel of Christ.

Paul said, "7 Even as it is meet for me to think this of you all, because I have you in my heart; inasmuch as both in my bonds, and in the defence and confirmation of the gospel, ye all are partakers of my grace. 17 But the other of love, knowing that I am set for the defence of the gospel" Phil 1:7, 17.

Paul said, "27 Only let your conversation be as it becometh the gospel of Christ: that whether I come and see you, or else be absent, I may hear of your affairs, that ye stand fast in one spirit, with one mind striving together for the faith of the gospel; 28 And in nothing terrified by your adversaries:

which is to them an evident token of perdition, but to you of salvation, and that of God" Phil 1:27-28.

Cult leaders and their gang members are some of the most manipulative and dangerous people in the religious world!

Gospel preachers: We must not become terrified by our adversaries: We must stand and teach the people of God, concerning the dangers that are in these false irreligious denominations.

Paul said, "14 That we henceforth be no more children, tossed to and fro, and carried about with every wind of doctrine, by the sleight of men, and cunning craftiness, whereby they lie in wait to deceive; 15 But speaking the truth in love, may grow up into him in all things, which is the head, even Christ" Eph 4:14-15.

Gospel preachers: We must continue to inform the people of the awful tragedy that took place in Jonestown, Guyana in 1978, where a Cult Leader causes over 900 people to commit suicide.

Gospel preachers: We must continue to inform the people of the awful tragedy that took place in Waco, Texas, in 1993, which was the most tragic incident in American religious history, where a religious Cult Leader caused 76 people to commit suicide.

The Black Hebrew Israelites: "Cult" teaches that their members must adopt a Hebrew name; to replace their birth names.

The Black Hebrew Israelites Cult Leaders: Demand that their members adopt a Hebrew name to replace their birth names which they say could have derived from slavery and they manipulate the minds of their members to believe that they are the only people that God will accept into Heaven.

The Bible: The word of God teaches that the members of the churches of Christ are called Christians.

Isaiah said, "1 For Zion's sake will I not hold my peace, and for Jerusalem's sake I will not rest, until the righteousness thereof go forth as brightness, and the salvation thereof as a lamp that burneth. 2 And the Gentiles shall see thy righteousness, and all kings thy glory: and thou shalt be called by a new name, which the mouth of the LORD shall name" Isaiah 62:1-2.

Paul said, "26 And when he had found him, he brought him unto Antioch. And it came to pass, that a whole year they assembled themselves with the church, and taught much people. And the disciples were called Christians first in Antioch" Acts 11:26.

The Black Hebrew Israelite Cult Leaders: Demand their members to become vegans: And to avoid any consumption of meat, dairy, eggs, and sugar.

The Bible: The word of God teaches that every creature of God *is* good.

Paul said, "4 For every creature of God is good, and nothing to be refused, if it be received with thanksgiving: 5 For it is sanctified by the word of God and prayer" 1 Tim 4:4-5.

Peter said, "7 And I heard a voice saying unto me, Arise, Peter; slay and eat. 8 But I said, Not so, Lord: for nothing common or unclean hath at any time entered into my mouth. 9 But the voice answered me again from heaven, What God hath cleansed, that call not thou common" Acts 11:7-9.

The Black Hebrew Israelites Cult Leaders: Teaches that polygamy is permitted **and** they forbid birth control. Their Leaders decide who will marry and whether marriage annulments will be permitted.

Paul said, "1 Know ye not, brethren, (for I speak to them that know the law,) how that the law hath dominion over a man as long as he liveth? 2 For the woman which hath an husband is bound by the law to her husband so long as he liveth; but if the husband be dead, she is loosed from the law of her husband" Romans 7:1-2.

Paul said, "1 Now concerning the things whereof ye wrote unto me: It is good for a man not to touch a woman. 2 Nevertheless, to avoid fornication, let every man have his own wife, and let every woman have her own husband. 3 Let the husband render unto the wife due benevolence: and likewise also the wife unto the husband" 1 Cor 7:1-3.

The Black Hebrew Israelites: Also call themselves Israel United in Christ (IUIC).

The Bible: The word of God teaches that, when believers get baptized into Christ they put on Christ.

Paul said, "3 Know ye not, that so many of us as were baptized into Jesus Christ were baptized into his death? 4 Therefore we are buried with him by baptism into death: that like as Christ was raised up from the dead by the glory of the Father, even so we also should walk in newness of life. 5 For if we have been planted together in the likeness of his death, we shall be also in the likeness of his resurrection" Romans 6:3-5.

Paul said, "26 For ye are all the children of God by faith in Christ Jesus. 27 For as many of you as have been baptized into Christ have put on Christ. 28 There is neither Jew nor Greek, there is neither bond nor free, there is neither male nor female: for ye are all one in Christ Jesus. 29 And if ye be Christ's, then are ye Abraham's seed, and heirs according to the promise" Gal 3:26-29.

The Black Hebrew Israelites Cult Leaders: Teaches that they are the only people that are going to heaven.

The Bible: The word of God teaches, that whosoever fear God and work righteousness is accepted with him.

The Bible said, "34 Then Peter opened his mouth, and said, Of a truth I perceive that God is no respecter of persons: 35 But in every nation he that feareth him, and worketh righteousness, is accepted with him" Acts 10:34-35.

Paul said, "14 For if we believe that Jesus died and rose again, even so them also which sleep in Jesus will God bring with him. 15 For this we say unto you by the word of the Lord, that we which are alive and remain unto the coming of the Lord shall not prevent them which are asleep. 16 For the Lord himself shall descend from heaven with a shout, with the voice of the archangel, and with the trump of God: and the dead in Christ shall rise first: 17 Then we which are alive and remain shall be caught up together with them in the clouds, to meet the Lord in the air: and so shall we ever be with the Lord. 18 Wherefore comfort one another with these words" 1 Thess 4:14-18.

Some Things That Christians Should Take Back From: The Devil

Christians Must Take Back: The Place Where God Said To Worship From The Devil.

When Covid-19 showed up in the world: Many congregations of the churches of Christ stop worshipping God in his house of Prayer.

The Bible said, "12 And the LORD appeared to Solomon by night, and said unto him, I have heard thy prayer, and have chosen this place to myself for an house of sacrifice. 13 If I shut up heaven that there be no rain, or if I command the locusts to devour the land, or if I send pestilence among my people; 14 If my people, which are called by my name, shall humble themselves, and pray, and seek my face, and turn from their wicked ways; then will I hear from heaven, and will forgive their sin, and will heal their land" 2 Chron 7:12-14.

God said, "7 Even them will I bring to my holy mountain, and make them joyful in my house of prayer: their burnt offerings and their sacrifices shall be accepted upon mine altar; for mine house shall be called an house of prayer for all people. 8 The Lord GOD which gathereth the outcasts of Israel saith, Yet will I gather others to him, beside those that are gathered unto him" Isaiah 56:7-8.

God said, "24 And in controversy they shall stand in judgment; and they shall judge it according to my judgments: and they shall keep my laws and my statutes in all mine assemblies; and they shall hallow my Sabbaths" Ezek 44:24.

The Bible said, "20 Our fathers worshipped in this mountain; and ye say, that in Jerusalem is the place where men ought to worship. 21 Jesus saith unto her, Woman, believe me, the hour cometh, when ye shall neither in this mountain, nor yet at Jerusalem, worship the Father. 22 Ye worship ye know not what: we know what we worship: for salvation is of the Jews. 23 But the hour cometh, and now is, when the true worshippers shall worship the Father in spirit and in truth: for the Father seeketh such to worship him. 24 God is a Spirit: and they that worship him must worship him in spirit and in truth" John 4:20-24.

When Covid-19 showed up in the world: Many Gospel Preachers gave the members of their congregations the permission to stay at home and worship God, this thing was totally a sin against God.

Jesus said, "13 But woe unto you, Scribes and Pharisees, Hypocrites! for ye Shut up the Kingdom of Heaven Against Men: for Ye Neither go in *Yourselves*, neither Suffer ye them that are entering to go In" Matt 23:13.

The Bible said, "7 And to the angel of the church in Philadelphia write; These things saith he that is holy, he that is true, he that hath the key of David, he that openeth, and no man shutteth; and shutteth, and no man openeth; 8 I know thy works: behold, I have set before thee an open door, and no man can shut it: for thou hast a little strength, and hast kept my word, and hast not denied my name" Rev 3:7-8.

The Bible said, "28 Whereupon the king took counsel, and made two calves of gold, and said unto them, It is too much for you to go up to Jerusalem: behold thy gods, O Israel, which brought thee up out of the land of Egypt. 29 And he set the one in Bethel, and the other put he in Dan. 30 And this thing became a sin: for the people went to worship before the one, even unto Dan" 1 Kings 12:28-30.

Gospel Preachers: We Must Take Back From The Devil: The Preaching Of The Gospel Of Christ Regardless To What He Put Us Through.

The Bible said, "27 And when they had brought them, they set them before the Council: and the High Priest asked them, 28 Saying, did not we Straitly Command You that ye should not Teach in this Name? and, behold, ye have filled Jerusalem with your Doctrine, and intend to bring this Man's Blood upon Us. 29 Then Peter and the Other Apostles answered and said, We ought to obey God rather than Men" Acts 5:27-29.

Paul said, "1 I charge thee therefore before God, and the Lord Jesus Christ, who shall judge the quick and the dead at his appearing and his kingdom; 2 Preach the word; be instant in season, out of season; reprove, rebuke, exhort with all longsuffering and doctrine. 3 For the time will come when they will not endure sound doctrine; but after their own lusts shall they heap to themselves teachers, having itching ears; 4 And they shall turn away their ears from the truth, and shall be turned unto fables. 5 But watch thou in all things, endure afflictions, do the work of an evangelist, make full proof of thy ministry" 2 Tim 4:1-5.

The Bible said, "34 Then stood there up one in the council, a Pharisee, named Gamaliel, a doctor of the law, had in reputation among all the people, and commanded to put the apostles forth a little space; 35 And said unto them, Ye men of Israel, take heed to yourselves what ye intend to do as touching these men. 36 For before these days rose up Theudas, boasting himself to be somebody; to whom a number of men, about four hundred, joined themselves: who was slain; and all, as many as obeyed him, were scattered, and brought to nought. 37 After this man rose up Judas of Galilee in the days of the taxing, and drew away much people after him: he also perished; and all, even as many as obeyed him, were dispersed. 38 And now I say unto you, Refrain from these men, and let them alone: for if this counsel or this work be of men, it will come to nought: 39 But if it be of God, ye cannot overthrow it; lest haply ye be found even to fight against God" Acts 5:34-39.

Paul said, "16 For I am not ashamed of the gospel of Christ: for it is the power of God unto salvation to every one that believeth; to the Jew first, and also to the Greek. 17 For therein is the righteousness of God revealed from faith to faith: as it is written, The just shall live by faith.

18 For the wrath of God is revealed from heaven against all ungodliness and unrighteousness of men, who hold the truth in unrighteousness; 19 Because that which may be known of God is manifest in them; for God hath shewed it unto them" Romans 1:16-19.

Paul said, "3 But if our Gospel be Hid, it is Hid to them that are Lost" 2 Cor 4:3.

Jesus said, "10 For the Son of man is come to seek and to save that which was lost" Luke 19:10.

When Covid-19 Showed up in the world: many gospel preachers fear the Devil and pervert the gospel of Christ.

John said, "17 Herein is our love made perfect, that we may have boldness in the day of judgment: because as he is, so are we in this world. 18 There is no fear in love; but perfect love casteth out fear: because fear hath torment. He that feareth is not made perfect in love. 19 We love him, because he first loved us" 1 John 4:17-19.

John said, "10 Fear none of those things which thou shalt suffer: behold, the devil shall cast some of you into prison, that ye may be tried; and ye shall have tribulation ten days: be thou faithful unto death, and I will give thee a crown of life. 11 He that hath an ear, let him hear what the Spirit saith unto the churches; He that overcometh shall not be hurt of the second death" Rev 2:10-11.

Paul said, "7 For God hath not given us the Spirit of Fear; but of Power, and of Love, and of a Sound Mind" 2 Tim 1:7.

Paul said, "6 I marvel that ye are so soon removed from him that called you into the grace of Christ unto another gospel: 7 Which is not another; but there be some that trouble you, and would pervert the gospel of Christ. 8 But though we, or an angel from heaven, preach any other gospel unto you than that which we have preached unto you, let him be accursed. 9 As we said before, so say I now again, If any man preach any other gospel unto you than that ye have received, let him be accursed. 10 For do I now persuade men, or God? or do I seek to please men? for if I yet pleased men, I should not be the servant of Christ. 11 But I certify you, brethren, that the gospel which was preached of me is not after man. 12 For I neither received it of man, neither was I taught it, but by the revelation of Jesus Christ" Gal 1:6-12.

The Bible said, "32 He that spared not his own Son, but delivered him up for us all, how shall he not with him also freely give us all things? 33 Who shall lay any thing to the charge of God's elect? It is God that justifieth. 34 Who is he that condemneth? It is Christ that died, yea rather, that is risen again, who is even at the right hand of God, who also maketh intercession for us. 35 Who shall separate us from the love of Christ? shall tribulation, or distress, or persecution, or famine, or nakedness, or peril, or sword? 36 As it is written, For thy sake we are killed all the day long; we are accounted as sheep for the slaughter. 37 Nay, in all these things we are more than conquerors through him that loved us. 38 For I am persuaded, that neither death, nor life, nor angels, nor principalities, nor powers, nor things present, nor things to come, 39 Nor height, nor depth, nor any other creature, shall be able to separate us from the love of God, which is in Christ Jesus our Lord" Romans 8:32-39.

Paul said, "16 For though I preach the gospel, I have nothing to glory of: for necessity is laid upon me; yea, woe is unto me, if I preach not the gospel! 17 For if I do this thing willingly, I have a reward: but if against my will, a dispensation of the gospel is committed unto me. 18 What is my reward then? Verily that, when I preach the gospel, I may make the gospel of Christ without charge, that I abuse not my power in the gospel" 1 Cor 9:16-18.

Illegal Use Of Alcohol And Drugs

Alcohol is: An Intoxicating Liquor.

Drugs are: An Intoxicating substance which comes in many difference forms.

Illegal use of Alcohol; can give people a false conception of their environment; it can cause people to become paranoid; which can cause people to harm and to kill others and themselves.

Illegal use of Drugs; can give people a false conception of their environment; it can cause people to become paranoid; which can cause people to harm and to kill others and themselves.

Illegal use of Alcohol and Drugs has caused many people to lose their families, their friends, their love ones, and even their own lives.

Men and Brethren: Let me make it absolutely clear, that God does not condone any Legal or Illegal use of intoxicating substances: Regardless to what the Food and Drug Administration has to say.

Strong Drinks: Are considered to be intoxicating.

The Bible said, "1 Wine is a mocker, strong drink is raging: and whosoever is deceived thereby is not wise" Prov 20:1.

Being under the Illegal use of Alcohol and or Drugs: Have fooled and influence many people to believe that they can perform rationally!

Solomon said, "4 It is not for kings, O Lemuel, it is not for kings to drink wine; nor for princes strong drink: 5 Lest they drink, and forget the law, and pervert the judgment of any of the afflicted. 6 Give strong drink unto him that is ready to perish, and wine unto those that be of heavy hearts. 7 Let him drink, and forget his poverty, and remember his misery no more" Prov 31:4-7.

Being under the influence of Alcohol and or Drugs: Has cause many people to forget their own actions or behavior.

The Bible said, "36 And Abigail came to Nabal; and, behold, he held a feast in his house, like the feast of a king; and Nabal's heart was merry within him, for he was very drunken: wherefore she told him nothing, less or more, until the morning light. 37 But it came to pass in the morning, when the wine was gone out of Nabal, and his wife had told him these things, that his heart died within him, and he became as a stone. 38 And it came to pass about ten days after, that the LORD smote Nabal, that he died"1 Sam 25:36-38.

Lot was intoxicated under the influence of Alcohol: And it caused him to get both of his daughters pregnant without him even knowing what he had done.

The Bible said, "30 And Lot went up out of Zoar, and dwelt in the mountain, and his two daughters with him; for he feared to dwell in Zoar: and he dwelt in a cave, he and his two daughters. 31 And the firstborn said unto the younger, Our father is old, and there is not a man in the earth to come in unto us after the manner of all the earth: 32 Come, let us make our father drink wine, and we will lie with him, that we may preserve seed of our father. 33 And they made their father drink wine that night: and the firstborn went in, and lay with her father; and he perceived not when she lay down, nor when she arose. 34 And it came to pass on the morrow, that the firstborn said unto the younger, Behold, I lay yesternight with my father: let us make him drink wine this night also; and go thou in, and lie with him, that we may preserve seed of our father. 35 And they made their father drink wine that night also: and the younger arose, and lay with him; and he perceived not when she lay down, nor when she arose" Gen 19:30-35.

The Devil has influence many people to believe that it is okay for them to drink intoxicating alcoholic drinks, or to use illegal drugs occasionally in the privacy of their homes: What these people need to realize is; that God's word apply even to people who are in the privacy of their homes.

Solomon said, "1 Wine is a mocker, strong drink is raging: and whosoever is deceived thereby is not wise" Prov 20:1.

There was a marriage in Cana of Galilee; and Jesus took water and made wine.

The Bible said, "1 And the third day there was a marriage in Cana of Galilee; and the mother of Jesus was there: 2 And both Jesus was called, and his disciples, to the marriage. 3 And when they wanted wine, the mother of Jesus saith unto him, They have no wine. 4 Jesus saith unto her, Woman, what have I to do with thee? mine hour is not yet come. 5 His mother saith unto the servants, Whatsoever he saith unto you, do it" John 2:1-5.

When the governor of the feast had tasted the water that was made wine; he recognized that that wine was not old fermented wine: you see new wine is not fermented; and it has a different taste.

The Bible said, "6 And there were set there six waterpots of stone, after the manner of the purifying of the Jews, containing two or three firkins apiece. 7 Jesus saith unto them, Fill the waterpots with water. And they filled them up to the brim. 8 And he saith unto them, Draw out now, and bear unto the governor of the feast. And they bare it. 9 When the ruler of the feast had tasted the water that was made wine, and knew not whence it was: (but the servants which drew the water knew;) the governor of the feast called the bridegroom, 10 And saith unto him, Every man at the beginning doth set forth good wine; and when men have well drunk, then that which is worse: but thou hast kept the good wine until now" John 2:6-10.

On the day of Pentecost; the people accused the Apostles of being intoxicated with new wine: Not knowing that new wine will not make people drunk.

The Bible said, "12 And they were all amazed, and were in doubt, saying one to another, What meaneth this? 13 Others mocking said, These men are full of new wine. 14 But Peter, standing up with the eleven, lifted up his voice, and said unto them, Ye men of Judaea, and all ye that dwell at Jerusalem, be this known unto you, and hearken to my words: 15 For these are not drunken, as ye suppose, seeing it is but the third hour of the day" Acts 2:12-15.

Jesus said, "39 No man also having drunk old wine straightway desireth new: for he saith, The old is better" Luke 5:39.

Men and Brethrens: My prayer to God is that those who have heard what the scriptures teach concerning alcohol, strong drinks, and illegal drugs that they will stop doing those things and turn to God for forgiveness.

The Bible said, "1 Wherefore seeing we also are compassed about with so great a cloud of witnesses, let us lay aside every weight, and the sin which doth so easily beset us, and let us run with patience the race that is set before us, 2 Looking unto Jesus the author and finisher of our faith; who for the joy that was set before him endured the cross, despising the shame, and is set down at the right hand of the throne of God. 3 For consider him that endured such contradiction of sinners against himself, lest ye be wearied and faint in your minds" Heb 12:1-3.

God's Instructions: For The Forgiveness Of Sin

God's Instructions: For the forgiveness of sin in the Old Testament Time.

God gave a 6 step Instruction: On how to forgive Rulers who have Sinned.

The Bible said, "22 When a Ruler hath Sinned, and done somewhat through ignorance against any of the commandments of the LORD his God concerning things which should not Be Done, and is Guilty; 23 Or if his sin, wherein he hath sinned, come to his knowledge; (**1**) he shall bring his offering, (**2**) a Kid of the Goats, (**3**) a Male without Blemish: 24 (**4**) And he shall lay his hand upon the head of the goat, and kill it in the place where they kill the burnt offering before the LORD: it is a sin offering. 25 (**5**) And the Priest shall take of the blood of the sin offering with his Finger, and put it upon the horns of the Altar of burnt offering, and shall pour out his Blood at the bottom of the altar of Burnt Offering. 26 And he shall burn All His Fat upon the Altar, as the fat of the sacrifice of peace offerings: (**6**) and the Priest shall make an Atonement for him as concerning his sin, and it shall be Forgiven Him" Lev 4:22-26.

God gave a 5 step Instruction: On how to forgive the common people that have sinned.

The Bible said, "27 And if any one of the Common People Sin through ignorance, while he doeth somewhat against any of the commandments of the LORD concerning things which ought not to be done, and be Guilty;

28 Or if his sin, which he hath sinned, come to his knowledge: then he shall bring his Offering, (**1**) a Kid of the Goats, a Female without Blemish, for his sin which he hath sinned. 29 (**2**) And he shall lay his hand upon the head of the sin offering, and slay the sin offering in the place of the burnt offering. 30 (**3**) And the Priest shall take of the Blood thereof with his finger, and put it upon the horns of the altar of burnt offering, and shall pour out all the blood thereof at the bottom of the altar. 31 And he shall take away all the fat thereof, as the fat is taken away from off the sacrifice of peace offerings; (**4**) and the priest shall burn it upon the altar for a sweet savour unto the LORD; (**5**) and the Priest shall make an Atonement for him, and it shall be Forgiven Him" Lev 4:27-31.

God gave a 3 step Instruction: On how to forgive a Congregation that has sinned.

The Bible said, "24 Then it shall be, if ought be committed by ignorance without the knowledge of the congregation, (**1**) that all the congregation shall offer one young bullock for a burnt offering, for a sweet savour unto the LORD, with his meat offering, and his drink offering, according to the manner, and one Kid of the Goats for a Sin Offering. 25 (**2**) And the Priest shall make an Atonement for all the congregation of the children of Israel, and it shall be forgiven them; for it is ignorance: (**3**) and they shall bring their offering, a sacrifice made by fire unto the LORD, and their sin offering before the LORD, for their ignorance: 26 And it shall be forgiven all the congregation of the children of Israel, and the stranger that sojourneth among them; seeing all the people were in ignorance" Num 15:24-26.

In The Old Testament: God said that he was going to make a New Covenant with his People.

The Bible said, "31 Behold, the days come, saith the LORD, that I will make a new covenant with the house of Israel, and with the house of Judah: 32 Not according to the covenant that I made with their fathers in the day that I took them by the hand to bring them out of the land of Egypt; which my covenant they brake, although I was an husband unto them, saith the LORD: 33 But this shall be the covenant that I will make with the house of Israel; After those days, saith the LORD, I will put my law in their inward parts, and write it in their hearts; and will be their God, and they shall be my people" Jer 31:31-33.

The Bible said, "8 For finding fault with them, he saith, Behold, the days come, saith the Lord, when I will make a new covenant with the house of Israel and with the house of Judah: 13 In that he saith, A new covenant, he hath made the first old. Now that which decayeth and waxeth old is ready to vanish away" Heb 8:8, 13.

God's Instructions: for the forgiveness of sin in the New Testament Time.

The Bible said, "24 And to Jesus the mediator of the new covenant, and to the blood of sprinkling, that speaketh better things than that of Abel" Heb 12:24.

God gave his people a different set of instructions for forgiveness in the New Testament; than he did in the Old Testament; and they were given by Jesus Christ.

Forgiveness: Is when a person have laid aside every, ought and every sin that someone have done against them in an irretrievable place in their mind; where they cannot retrieve them ever again.

The Bible said, "1 Wherefore seeing we also are compassed about with so great a cloud of witnesses, let us lay aside every weight, and the sin which doth so easily beset us, and let us run with patience the race that is set before us, 2 Looking unto Jesus the author and finisher of our faith; who for the joy that was set before him endured the cross, despising the shame, and is set down at the right hand of the throne of God" Heb 12:1-2.

Jesus gave a 5 step Instruction: On how to forgive a Brother who has sinned against his Brother.

Jesus said, "23 Therefore if thou bring thy gift to the altar, and there rememberest that thy Brother hath Ought Against Thee; 24 **(1)** Leave

There Thy Gift before the Altar, **(2)** and Go Thy Way; **(3)** First be Reconciled to thy Brother, **(4)** and then come and offer thy gift. 25 **(5)** Agree with thine Adversary Quickly, whiles thou art in the way with him; lest at any time the adversary deliver thee to the judge, and the judge deliver thee to the officer, and thou be cast into prison. 26 Verily I say unto thee, Thou shalt by no means come out thence, till thou hast paid the uttermost farthing" Matt 5:23-26.

Jesus gave a 4 step Instruction: On how to forgive a Brother who has sinned against His Brother.

Jesus said, "15 Moreover if thy brother shall trespass against thee, **(1)** go and tell him his fault between thee and him alone: if he shall hear thee, thou hast gained thy brother. 16 But if he will not hear thee, **(2)** then take with thee one or two more, that in the mouth of two or three witnesses every word may be established. 17 **(3)** And if he shall neglect to hear them, tell it unto the church: **(4)** but if he neglect to hear the church, let him be unto thee as an heathen man and a publican" Matt 18:15-17.

Jesus gave a 4 step Instruction: On how to forgive a Brother who have sinned against another Brother.

Jesus said, "3 Take heed to yourselves: If thy brother trespass against thee, **(1)** rebuke him; **(2)** and if he repent, **(3)** forgive him. 4 And if he trespass against thee seven times in a day, and seven times in a day turn again to thee, **(4)** saying, I repent; thou shalt forgive him. 5 And the apostles said unto the Lord, Increase our faith" Luke 17:3-5.

Paul gave a 5 step Instruction: On how to forgive a Brother who has been overtaken in a fault.

Paul said, "1 Brethren, if a man be overtaken in a fault, **(1)** ye which are spiritual, **(2)** restore such an one **(3)** in the spirit of meekness; **(4)** considering thyself, **(5)** lest thou also be tempted" Gal 6:1.

Paul gave a 1 step Instruction: On how to forgive a Congregation that has sinned.

Paul said, "20 **(1)** Them that sin rebuke before all, that others also may fear. 21 I charge thee before God, and the Lord Jesus Christ, and the elect angels, that thou observe these things without preferring one before another, doing nothing by partiality" 1 Tim 5:20-21.

During the days of the Apostles: James gave a 4 step Instruction: On how to forgive a sick member of a Congregation.

James said, "14 Is any sick among you? **(1)** let him call for the elders of the church; **(2)** and let them pray over him, **(3)** anointing him with oil in the name of the Lord: 15 And the prayer of faith shall save the sick, and the Lord shall raise him up; and if he have committed sins, they shall be forgiven him. 16 **(4)** Confess your faults one to another, and pray one for another, that ye may be healed. The effectual fervent prayer of a righteous man availeth much" James 5:14-16.

Jesus Explained; the crucial importance to the people of God, concerning why we should forgive one another; In a 5 step Instruction!

Jesus said, "9 **(1)** After this manner therefore pray ye: Our Father which art in heaven, Hallowed be thy name. 10 Thy kingdom come. Thy will be done in earth, as it is in heaven. 11 Give us this day our daily bread. 12 **(2)** And forgive us our debts, as we forgive our debtors. 13 **(3)** And lead us not into temptation, but deliver us from evil: For thine is the kingdom, and the power, and the glory, for ever. Amen. 14 **(4)** For if ye forgive men their trespasses, your heavenly Father will also forgive you: 15 **(5)** But if ye forgive not men their trespasses, neither will your Father forgive your trespasses" Matt 6:9-15.

The Devil Wants To Deceive The Entire World To Believe, That The Great Commission That Christ Gave To His Twelve Disciples Was Given To All Gospel Preachers Who Live In All Of The Continents Of The World; And That Is Absolutely A False Deception.

After Christ's resurrection from the dead, he gave his twelve Disciples a command to go into the entire world and teach mankind to become Disciples of Christ, during that particular time Asia was the only continent in the world.

The Bible said, "1 And when he had called unto him his twelve Disciples, he gave them power against unclean spirits, to cast them out, and to heal all manner of sickness and all manner of disease. 2 Now the names of the twelve apostles are these; The first, Simon, who is called Peter, and Andrew his brother; James the son of Zebedee, and John his brother; 3 Philip, and Bartholomew; Thomas, and Matthew the publican; James the son of Alphaeus, and Lebbaeus, whose surname was Thaddaeus; 4 Simon the Canaanite, and Judas Iscariot, who also betrayed him" Matt 10:1-4.

The Bible said, "18 And Jesus came and spake unto them, saying, All power is given unto me in heaven and in earth. 19 Go ye therefore, and teach all nations, baptizing them in the name of the Father, and of the Son, and of the Holy Ghost: 20 Teaching them to observe all things whatsoever I have commanded you: and, lo, I am with you alway, even unto the end of the world. Amen" Matt 28:18-20.

There are many gospel preachers and religious people in the world today who do not understand that those Twelve Disciples that Christ sent into the entire world to preach the gospel to every creature did exactly what Christ commanded them to do. You see, during the days of the apostles, the Continent of Asia was the entire world.

The Bible said, "16 But they have not all obeyed the gospel. For Esaias saith, Lord, who hath believed our report? 17 So then faith cometh by hearing, and hearing by the word of God. 18 But I say, Have they not heard? Yes verily, their sound went into all the earth, and their words unto the ends of the world" Romans 10:16-18.

Men and Brethren; It would be so remarkable; if all gospel preachers and all of the Disciples of Christ who live in every continent of the world would go into their highways, into their streets, and into their country lanes and gathered together as many as they could find and bring them into the church of Christ and fill it up: With that; God will be well pleased.

The Bible said, "8 Then saith he to his servants, The wedding is ready, but they which were bidden were not worthy. 9 Go ye therefore into the highways, and as many as ye shall find, bid to the marriage. 10 So those servants went out into the highways, and gathered together all as many as they found, both bad and good: and the wedding was furnished with guests" Matt 22:8-10.

Paul said, "16 For I am not ashamed of the gospel of Christ: for it is the power of God unto salvation to every one that believeth; to the Jew first, and also to the Greek. 17 For therein is the righteousness of God revealed from faith to faith: as it is written, The just shall live by faith" Romans 1:16-17.

Prayer Of Thanks

Paul said, "1 I exhort therefore, that, first of all, supplications, prayers, intercessions, and giving of thanks, be made for all men; 2 For kings, and for all that are in authority; that we may lead a quiet and peaceable life in all godliness and honesty. 3 For this is good and acceptable in the sight of God our Saviour; 4 Who will have all men to be saved, and to come unto the knowledge of the truth. 5 For there is one God, and one mediator between God and men, the man Christ Jesus" 1 Tim 2:1-5.

My Prayer to God is: That through the reading of this book; that all believers will become stronger in the Lord; and that all unbelievers will become believers in the Lord.

Paul said, "15 For in Christ Jesus neither circumcision availeth any thing, nor uncircumcision, but a new creature. 16 And as many as walk according to this rule, peace be on them, and mercy, and upon the Israel of God. 17 From henceforth let no man trouble me: for I bear in my body the marks of the Lord Jesus" Gal 6:15-17.

Paul said, "15 And let the peace of God rule in your hearts, to the which also ye are called in one body; and be ye thankful. 16 Let the word of Christ dwell in you richly in all wisdom; teaching and admonishing one another in psalms and hymns and spiritual songs, singing with grace in your hearts to the Lord. 17 And whatsoever ye do in word or deed, do all in the name of the Lord Jesus, giving thanks to God and the Father by him" Col 3:15-17.

David said, "1 I waited patiently for the LORD; and he inclined unto me, and heard my cry. 2 He brought me up also out of an horrible pit, out of the miry clay, and set my feet upon a rock, and established my goings. 3 And he hath put a new song in my mouth, even praise unto our God: many shall see it, and fear, and shall trust in the LORD. 4 Blessed is that man that maketh the LORD his trust, and respecteth not the proud, nor such as turn aside to lies" Psalms 40:1-4.

I am truly thankful to all of you for reading my books: And for viewing our videos on YouTube: And I hope that you will help us to spread the gospel of Christ, by telling your family and your friends to read my books, and to view our videos on YouTube and subscribe. Thank you.

You can view us on YouTube at: The North Little Rock Church Of Christ, You can also view us on YouTube by Scanning Our QR Code On Your Cell Phone.

www.ingramcontent.com/pod-product-compliance
Lightning Source LLC
Chambersburg PA
CBHW061735070526
44585CB00024B/2681